The Manatee Murders

By

John D. Mills

ISBN: 0-7596-5434-4

This book is printed on acid free paper.

1stBooks - rev. 10/11/01

This book is dedicated to the preservation of the manatee and Florida boaters.

This is a work of fiction. Names, characters, places, and incidents either are the product of the author's imagination or are used fictitiously, and any resemblance to actual persons, living or dead, business establishments, events, or locales is entirely coincidental.

Detective Doug Shearer is awakened from his sleep with terrible news—three beheaded manatees are floating in Pine Island Sound. A local commercial fisherman is arrested, but there are other, unknown people involved. Doug attempts to solve the crime with the help of prosecutor Roger Barklett. While investigating the crime, Doug's personal life is turned into a shambles when his ex-flame decides she wants him back. Sit back and enjoy the ride as Doug Shearer tries to solve the manatee murders.

Read what the critics wrote about John D. Mills's first book,

Reasonable and Necessary

"Mills knows how to tell a story...Readers who consider Grisham and Turow to be the standard bearers of the legal thriller should find Mills's work enjoyable and worthwhile."

Happenings magazine

"an exceptional talent...moves the plot along swiftly with a refreshingly wry humor."

Island Sun News

"a fast-paced and lively novel that touches a lot of hot button issues without being preachy."

Lehigh Star

Author's Acknowledgments

I am very grateful to the following people that read my original manuscript and offered ideas for improvement:

Professor Russell Franklin
JoEllen Kane
Amy Anthony
Doug Wilkinson
Bruce Oliphant
Gail Lawson
Wendy Resh
John Shearer
Hal Stevens
Joy Mills
Lisa Fasig
Terri Hendricks
Marianne Boos
Greg Rasmussen
Clint Busbee

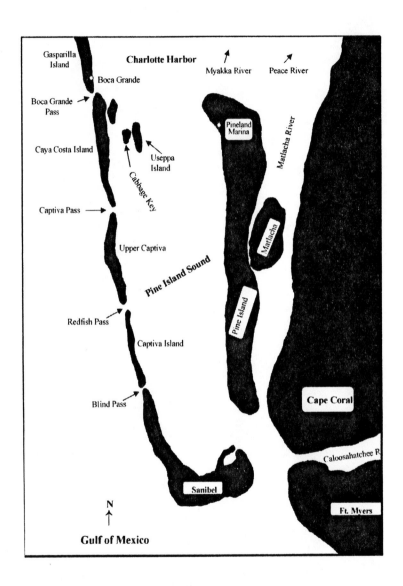

Gasparilla
Island

Charlotte Harbor

Myakka River   Peace River

Boca Grande

Boca Grande
Pass

Caya Costa Island

Pineland
Marina

Useppa
Island

Matlacha River

Cabbage Key

Captiva Pass

Upper Captiva

Matlacha

Pine Island Sound

Pine Island

Redfish Pass

Captiva Island

Cape Coral

Blind Pass

Caloosahatchee R.

Sanibel

N

Ft. Myers

Gulf of Mexico

Chapter 1

The bald man smiled as he saw the white floats on his gill net splashing together in the froth created by the struggling manatee. The silver-haired man pulled the throttle back and his twin outboard engines slowed to a steady purr as his spotlight lit up the trap they had set earlier that moonless night.

"We got her now. She's all tangled up with the net and that radio buoy on her back. We just have to pull her in closer and tie the weightline to the cleat. After that she's done," the bald man yelled in a triumphant tone.

The silver-haired man started laughing and said "I wish all those manatee lovers could see how their beloved manatee got trapped in our net because of that radio buoy they attached to her to monitor her movements."

The bald man pulled in the net that they secured two hours ago at high tide across a mangrove-lined creek mouth in the Ding Darling Sanctuary on Sanibel Island. Their Global Positioning Satellite (GPS) monitor, interfaced with the onboard computer, allowed them to track the manatee. They knew from the manatee sites on the Internet that the manatee they were tracking was a 14-foot mature female with some barnacle growth on her head.

Two hours before, they had motored up the creek about two hundred yards from the trap they set and anchored their 24-foot Grady-White. They smelled the decaying mangrove leaves as they drank beer and talked about the latest gossip on the islands in the darkness of the deserted creek. As the tide flowed out of the creek, they waited for the manatee as the mosquitoes bit their necks and ears. After they consumed a twelve pack, the distinctive nostril blow of a manatee breathing was easily heard. They waited until the big manatee passed them and they pulled the anchor and started the engines. The creek was about 30 feet wide and their depth finder showed it was ten feet deep. The boat followed the manatee but with the falling tide it couldn't go up into the mangrove roots to get away from the loud boat. The only way for the manatee to escape the noise was to swim to the mouth of the creek. Since the manatee was young, she had been taught by her family members to stay away from boats. She swam faster with the tide to get away from the sound coming up behind her. She didn't see the net until it was too late. She struggled to swim under the net weights on the sandy bottom, but the radio buoy attached to her back by a tether cord became snagged in the net. She instinctively began turning and the net became tighter around her with every turn.

The bald man pulled the weightline of the net that trapped the manatee next to the boat. She bounced up against the boat, using her failing strength to slowly move her flume in a futile escape attempt. As the bald man secured the net on the rear cleat of the boat he said, "She's ready. Make sure you put it close so the sound is muffled."

The silver-haired man loaded his 12-gauge shotgun with a single shell. He leaned over the edge of his boat pointing the barrel between the eyes of the manatee and pushed the barrel into the thick flesh. He paused briefly as the floodlight above the cutty cabin caught the face of the manatee and caused her to blink. He thought he saw a tear falling from her right eye, but he quickly dismissed it as his imagination. The muffled shotgun blast sprayed flesh and blood all over the outside of the boat and on the silver-haired man.

The bald man picked some of the manatee flesh off of the silver-haired man's shirt and ate it. The bald man laughed and said, "Manatee sushi! It tastes pretty good. Kind of like bald eagle, but more chewy."

The lifeless body of the manatee floated in the bloody water next to the boat. From the edge of the mangrove roots they heard another distinctive manatee blow and shined the spotlight up towards the sound. A baby manatee was slowly swimming towards them and her trapped, lifeless mother.

The silver-haired man shouted, "This is a bonus! Grab the speargun."

Chapter 2

Doug Shearer awoke from a deep sleep when his beeper went off. As he reached over to his nightstand and turned on the lamp, he slowly remembered he had beeper duty for the week for any major crimes that required a detective. His clock showed it was 2 a.m. and his mind told him through the fogginess he'd been asleep for three hours. His stiff body ached as he dragged himself to the bathroom to relieve himself and splash water on his face to wake up.

After his morning ritual, he called the shift supervisor at the Lee County Sheriff's Office. After going through the switchboard, Doug was put through.

"Doug, we've got a weird one out on Captiva. The marine patrol saw an unlit boat in Roosevelt Channel behind 'Tween Waters Inn and then shined their spotlight and approached. The driver cut a rope from his boat and tried to get away by leaving something big floating in the water. They drove up to it and saw it was a dead manatee with his head missing. They were able to catch the boat and apprehend the driver. Some local commercial fisherman, Buck Williams. Have you heard of 'em?"

Doug swallowed hard as he realized one of the patriarchs of a Matlacha fishing family was in serious trouble and he said slowly, "Yeah, I know him; his son and I went to high school. He's in his late sixties. Why would he kill and behead a manatee?"

The shift supervisor replied, "I don't know. But we've got a mess and we want to make sure the investigation is done right. I thought that since you lived in Matlacha, Mr. Williams might talk to you. So far he's invoked his right to remain silent and we can't get anything out of him. All we've got is a 12-foot beheaded manatee, an old mullet skiff with a bloody chain saw and an old, crusty fisherman who won't say nothin'."

Doug answered, "Have the deputies on the scene bring him to the interview room at the main office and I'll meet you there in an hour. Hav'em tell Mr. Williams that I'm gonna be there to talk to him."

Doug dragged himself to the shower and turned on the hot water. As the bathroom steamed up, he brushed his teeth and thought about Buck Williams. Buck was in his late sixties but looked older. A lifetime of commercial fishing in the brutal Southwest Florida sun had taken its toll. There were sunspots up and down his muscular forearms and assorted pockmarks on his face and neck from having cancer spots removed. So far he had dodged any fatal, malignant spots but the odds were catching up to him.

The last time he had seen Buck in person was at his wife's funeral last year. Buck and his wife had their fiftieth wedding anniversary the week before she died of a heart attack. At the viewing, the night before the funeral, Doug watched Buck cry uncontrollably in the front pew of the chapel at the funeral home. Buck was seated ten feet away from the casket, looking at it while crying loudly. It was almost as if he were scared to look at his wife's body. After an hour of staring at the casket, he stood and slowly approached. Doug watched in disbelief as Buck started to climb into the casket with his dead wife. He rushed forward with Buck's son, Carl, and pulled him back to the standing position. Doug had never forgotten the grieved look on Buck's rugged face as he had whispered in a strange voice, "Let me go. I'm going with her."

Doug and Carl calmed him down and brought him back to the front pew. The next day at the funeral Buck reacted totally different. He didn't cry a tear. He just stared stoically at the preacher giving the eulogy. After the ceremony Carl quietly led him away to an awaiting car. Doug had heard that Buck hadn't been doing well since the funeral.

An hour later Doug walked into the sheriff's office and saw a crowd gathered outside the interview room. Doug called Sgt.

John D. Mills

Sally Gardner, the crime scene investigator, on his cell phone. She answered on the third ring, "Hello, this is Gardner."

"Sally, this is Doug. I'm down at the station and getting ready to interview the defendant. Can you tell me what you've found so far?"

"Not much. The manatee heads are nowhere to be found. There's a bunch of rope in the bottom of his boat. A lot more than he used on this manatee. All we have for a weapon is this chainsaw. He must be talented as hell if he can lasso a moving manatee and hold it still with one hand, while cutting its head off with the other."

Doug considered her point and said, "It is sort of amazing, isn't it. I'll make sure and ask him about it. Thanks for your help, Sally."

"No problem. I'll call if anything comes up. Goodbye."

Doug confirmed with the shift supervisor that Buck knew he was coming to talk to him. Doug took a deep breath, opened the door and walked into the brightly-lit, 12' by 10', cream-colored room. He saw Buck sitting at a small metal table smoking a cigarette and said, "Hello, Mr. Williams. How are you doing tonight?"

Buck smiled and stood up as Doug approached with his hand extended. He put his cigarette down in the ashtray and said, "I'm doing O.K. The people here 'ave been real nice to me, Doug. Gave me cigarettes and hot coffee."

Doug and Buck sat down at the table and looked at each other. Doug noticed that Buck appeared to have shrunk since he saw him at the funeral. His fingers were slowly cramping inwards at different angles. The veins on his face were visible through his tanned, dried-out skin, and the Adam's apple in his throat was slightly shaking. He was still dressed in his smelly fishing clothes.

"Mr. Williams, I guess you know why you're here. They found ya with a dead, headless manatee. Is there anything ya want to tell me? If ya do, I need to read ya your rights."

6

Buck shifted in his chair and looked down at the table, "Doug, I don't want ta be rude, but I's told not ta say anything. I'll talk ta you about anything but this mess with the manatee."

Doug looked closely at Buck and sensed his embarrassment. He hesitated and said, "Mr. Williams, who told ya not to say anything?"

Buck looked down and said, "I'm sorry, Doug. I know you're just doin' ya job, but I can't say anything else."

Doug said goodbye and left the interview room bewildered by Buck Williams' actions and demeanor. By the time he completed his report, checked out and returned to his Ford pickup, dawn was lightening the eastern sky. Doug drove home to Matlacha in a daze as he pondered the dead manatee. Buck was no angel but he would never kill a fish or animal except to eat it or sell it to the market for others to eat. Thirty minutes later as Doug drove over the Matlacha bridge he watched one of the regular fisherman fighting a large snook. The sun was now a fiery reddish-orange, and it sliced through the cloudless morning as he parked his truck in his driveway. Doug was tired but knew that he was too wound up to sleep, so he decided to get his morning workout done.

Doug alternated jogging and swimming six days a week and rested on the seventh. Today was his jogging day, so he went inside and dressed out. After stretching, he started on a slow pace down the dirt road towards the boat ramp. Doug did some of his best thinking while exercising. However, today was different. All he could think of was the picture of the headless manatee floating in the dark water. After his four-mile jog, Doug slowed down in front of his house and walked slowly to cool down.

Doug's house was one of the old cracker houses built on a canal by a commercial fisherman. The inside was cypress wood that had been sanded perfectly and left to age with no sealant. It still produced a rich smell, and the color of the wood softened the overhead lights. The outside wood was a hodge-podge of different wood that the previous owner had covered over with

7

white siding. The roof was tin and efficiently reflected the brutal Florida sun. The bathroom was pieced together with a cream colored bathtub, beige sink and white commode. His kitchen had an old refrigerator, gas stove, and sink. He had air conditioning units in his windows and each room had an overhead wooden fan. His driveway was made of white shell and sand that led to an outdoor carport.

As Doug was cooling down, a flock of pelicans flew over his canal heading into the wind at a slow pace. The morning humidity was stifling so Doug went inside and got a nice cold shower. After drying off and drinking a cold glass of water, he fell onto his bed and quickly fell asleep.

Chapter 3

The telephone ringing woke Doug up at noon after a short two hour nap. Against his body's advice, Doug climbed out of bed and answered his phone with a groggy hello.

"Wake up sleepyhead, we've got work to do," a perky Roger Barklett chided.

Roger was one of Doug's original friends from when he had joined the sheriff's office 12 years ago. Roger was a prosecutor with the State Attorney's office and they had worked on many cases over the years and become close.

Doug replied slowly, "Roger, give me a break. I was up all night workin' that manatee killing with Buck Williams."

"That's why I'm calling. There are now three dead manatees. The one behind 'Tween Waters was the first. A second was found this morning by a fisherman outside of Ding Darling Sanctuary, in the mouth of McIntire creek. The third was found by a tourist on the main dirt road through Ding Darling. It was a baby manatee impaled on a mangrove branch next to the road. All of 'em were headless."

The news of the additional killings shocked Doug into full consciousness, sending adrenaline pumping through his body. He silently cursed Buck Williams for not telling him about the other manatees. He hesitated before asking, "So what's your boss want us to do?"

"He wants to make sure all of the evidence has been collected properly and the case worked up ASAP. I've been assigned the case and he wants a fast trial of this bastard. The media is all over this. Channel 5 has set up a broadcast in Ding Darling Sanctuary and there are so many damn news helicopters flying over Pine Island Sound it looks like a flock of vultures. The *Save Our Seacows* club is having a press conference at 2:00 p.m. at the Punta Rassa boat ramp. I don't guess they'll miss a chance to condemn the boaters as the cause of all the problems."

Doug answered, "I sent the body of the first manatee to the lab for a necropsy to see if there was any evidence. I called in the dive team to look for the head of the manatee where the first carcass was found. I'll call them and send them to the new spots, also. I'll call my lab people and have them send the other two carcasses out for a necropsy. I've talked to the defendant but he doesn't want to make a statement. I'm not sure what else to do. Any suggestions?"

Roger thought for moment before answering, "I can't think of anything else right now but let me talk to the bigwigs and see what they think. Meanwhile, why don't you turn on channel 5 and see all of the good publicity we're getting. The chamber of commerce people must be pulling their hair out."

Doug said goodbye and turned on the TV. The first thing he noticed was the subtitle at the bottom of the screen. In blood red letters, the caption read *The Manatee Murders*. The reporter was giving the background information on the crime and the importance of the manatee. She then interviewed the president and founder of *Save Our Seacows*, George Steinworth IV. He gave a polished presentation that the manatee, also known as a seacow in different countries, was a gentle creature that was not a threat and called for life in prison for Buck Williams. Steinworth then opined that he was sure that the boaters were behind the killings because they were upset with the new manatee speed zones. He called for more slow speed zones and increased enforcement.

Doug became angry as he listened to Steinworth irresponsibly slander all local boaters. Doug's father and grandfather had been commercial fishermen, and Doug had owned a fishing boat ever since he was an adult. He respected manatees along with most boaters and he was tired of being accused of causing manatee deaths. Now to hear George Steinworth slander him and all of his friends on TV was too much.

Doug showered, dressed and ate breakfast while flipping through the channels and watching the reports on the manatee killings. All of the media were now calling them *The Manatee Murders*. After breakfast, Doug got into his old Ford pickup and drove to work while listening to his favorite country music station.

When Doug arrived at the sheriff's office, his secretary stared at him with wide eyes as she was talking on the phone. Doug picked up his dozen messages and realized the media had found out he was involved in the manatee investigation and wanted interviews. When his secretary got off the phone she said, "They want to see you down at the big office. Apparently they sacrificed you as point man for this manatee fiasco. Good luck."

Doug's head pounded as he walked down the hall to the administration wing of the Emerald Palace. A prior sheriff ordered all of the outside walls at the sheriff's office painted green. Someone had dubbed it the Emerald Palace and the name had stuck. Doug walked into the conference room and saw all of his supervisors staring at him. His lieutenant spoke up, "Doug, glad you could make it. We've been thinking about you being in charge of this manatee situation. You have a boat and know all of the waters. You know the defendant and might be able to develop some leads that some of our city-slicker boys might not be able to. Since you're the detective in charge, we figured you should handle the press."

Doug smiled at everyone and realized that no matter what he said, his fate was already sealed. He didn't really want to know the answer but asked anyway, "What do you want me to do first?"

His lieutenant gave his best fake smile and said, "The press conference starts in five minutes. You better go down the hall and get on the radio for the latest updates."

Doug walked into the communications room and called Sgt. Gardner on the radio. After a few seconds she answered, "Gardner here. What do you need Doug?"

"I've been elected to handle the press conference. Anything new I should know?"

"We found a cell phone in the bilge of the boat. It was still on but sitting in salt water, so I doubt we can get anything from it, but we're sending it in for tests. Other than that, nothing new."

"Thanks, Sally. 10-4."

"10-4."

Doug walked down to the pressroom and entered the loud room filled with hungry reporters. As he was walking up to the podium, five different reporters started asking questions. Doug put up his hand and said, "Ladies and Gentlemen, I first have a few comments and then I will answer your questions. This morning, one of our marine patrol units was responding to phoned-in complaint of illegal net fishing on the bay side of Captiva. When he arrived, he saw a fisherman in an unlit boat fleeing from him. As he investigated the scene, he found a dead, headless manatee. He gave chase and captured the fisherman, who we have in custody. A few hours later, two other dead, headless manatees were found in the same area.

"At this time, I will answer any questions you might have."

A man with slicked back hair and a yellow bow tie blurts out, "Can you give us an estimate of how big the heads were and your guess on where they are located?"

Doug hesitated and then said, "There were two adult female heads and a baby. I have no idea what happened to the heads."

"Do these killings have some symbolism for any Indian religions?"

Doug was flustered but blurted out, "I have no idea if there is any connection to a religious cult and Indian religion."

Doug stood at the podium answering equally ridiculous questions for fifty minutes. After a confrontational afternoon of weird questions with all of the local reporters, Doug was more than happy to leave the Emerald Palace at 3:30 p.m. Even though he was tired, Doug was excited because his boat was finally getting out of the shop after four months of refurbishing.

The first three months it had been at Cullen Sander's shop getting a makeover. Doug had set aside $15,000 of the money he had inherited from his best friend, Sandy. He used this money for a new engine and used the remaining $335,000 to set up a college scholarship for children of Boca Grande fishing guides. Sandy's father, Big Papa, had been excited when Doug told him about his decision.

Doug decided that if he was going to put a new engine on his old 20-foot Mako, he might as well spend some more money and fix all of his nicks and cracks in his fiberglass hull. Cullen talked him into having the old yellow gel coat stripped down and repainted white. It had taken Cullen three months between his regular fishing trips to finish the work.

Doug missed Sandy terribly so he decided to name his refinished boat *Two Tongues*. Doug had fond memories of his time with former best friend, Sandy, on the original *Two Tongues* before it had been intentionally blown up by a hitman hired by crooked insurance executives. They were never prosecuted but Doug had made sure justice was served.

Doug called his friend Tom at *The Sign Guys* in Lehigh Acres and he designed blue 8" high letters with a gold border around them. When he had picked the newly named boat up, a broad smile crossed his face as he thought of the good times on the original *Two Tongues.* But his face turned pale as he thought of Sandy's violent death.

Doug got a good deal from Scotty at *San Carlos Marine* on a 225 Yamaha V-Max engine. After the engine was mounted, Doug took the *Two Tongues* to Craig at *Smith Marine.* Craig put on a new trolling motor and outfitted the *Two Tongues* with all the latest bells and whistles: a 3-D color depth finder, GPS system and, of course, AM/FM radio with CD player. It took Craig a month to do the work because he was usually fishing with Cullen.

The *Two Tongues* was totally new except for the hull. The hull was better than new. The older fiberglass hulls were much better than the new "space age" technology hulls because they were made with more layers of fiberglass and more "hands-on" care before mass-produced, cookie-cutter hulls cheapened the product. Doug doubted that any of the Space Shuttles had ever taken on a November nor'wester coming across Charlotte Harbor.

It was the first Friday afternoon in March and an eastern breeze cooled the sunny afternoon. Doug smiled as he was riding down U.S. 41 in his old Ford pickup with the windows down—he could feel the coming spring in his blood. He thought of all the hungry snook that would begin hitting any available bait in the Caloosahatchee River. Doug was stopping by *Smith Marine* to finally pick up his newly christened *Two Tongues*. As Doug pulled into *Smith Marine* he saw a *U.S. Fish and Wildlife* boat being trailered behind a white Dodge pickup with the corresponding emblem painted on the door parked out front.

Craig met Doug as he parked his truck and said, "Well, your boat's ready—that's the good news. The bad news is that there might not be too many places to use it. Our buddy with *Fish and Wildlife* stopped by to have his boat serviced today and told us that his bosses up in Washington are really pissed off about these dead manatees. They just might put an emergency moratorium on boats using Pine Island Sound and Matlacha River to show us locals they ain't intimidated by our terrorist tactics."

Doug looked incredulously at Craig and slowly realized by his stern look that he wasn't kidding. Doug closed his eyes and rubbed them as he realized his bad dream had just gotten worse.

Chapter 4

Doug met Roger at the jail for the bond hearing on Buck's case the following morning at 10:00 a.m. They walked into the small, smelly first appearance room just off of the jail lobby. The prisoners were lined up in a fenced-in area with bailiffs giving directions. On one side of the fence Judge Nathaniel Hill, clerks, prosecutors and police sat closely together reading over the arrest reports and making recommendations before the judge set a bond. On the other side of the fence, a young public defender sat by herself and gallantly fought for a low bond for her new clients. It was good training for the public defender. She learned to lose her arguments gracefully while the chummy group on the other side of the fence did what they wanted to do.

Judge Hill called all of the other cases first, allowing the reporters plenty of time to assemble in an adjacent room and watch the bond hearing via a TV monitor. He finally bellowed out, "Mr. Buck Williams, please step forward."

Buck was still dressed in his dirty fishing clothes he had on when arrested. The poignant smell of dried out fish slime, manatee blood and human perspiration produced an invisible gaseous cloud that moved whenever Buck did. The clerks politely covered their noses with tissues when Buck moved closer, but Judge Hill was determined not to show any reaction to Buck's odor.

Judge Hill spoke in his most somber voice, "Does the state have a recommendation for bond?"

Roger stepped in front of the young prosecutor that had been waiting for the chance to let loose with a verbal barrage in front of the media that was searching for a sound bite for the evening news. Roger spoke in a clean, crisp manner, "Your honor, because of the savage butchery in this case, and the fact that there were three manatees killed and beheaded, were are asking for a $300,000 bond."

15

Judge Hill slowly looked towards the public defender and asked, "Does the public defender have a comment?"

The young public defender swallowed hard, took a deep breath and said, "Your honor, my client has informed me that he is going to hire a private attorney. However, for this hearing I would like to point out a few things. He has a no prior felonies. His only crimes are alcohol-related misdemeanors such as disorderly conduct, open containers, and breach of the peace. We're asking that he be released on his own recognizance."

Judge Hill pretended to be reading the arrest report as he silently practiced his speech. After a pregnant pause of seven seconds, he looked Buck in the eyes and forcefully said, "The allegations against you are terrible and disturbing to a civilized society. If you are convicted of these crimes, you will be looking at serious prison time. Because that makes you a flight risk, I'm setting the bond at $300,000."

As Roger and Doug left the first appearance room, the media pounced on them in the lobby.

"How high was the bond?"

"Did the defendant confess?"

"Who does he have for lawyer?"

"What did they do with the heads?"

Doug and Roger patiently answered the questions. When the press realized that there was no new information, they slowly left the lobby. Doug's headache was getting worse by the minute.

Chapter 5

Doug woke up early and got *Two Tongues* ready for the day's trip. His day's assignment wasn't bad. Roger was coming out to Doug's and they were going to cruise to where the manatee carcasses were found while discussing trial strategy. It had been a week since the manatee carcasses were found and they still hadn't come up with a motive. They had worked on many cases together and sent some bad people to prison. Doug truly felt like he was making a difference when he got evil people off the street. But with Buck, he just didn't understand why he was involved in this bizarre crime.

Doug's canal in Matlacha opened towards the east into the Matlacha River. Doug looked down to the mouth of his canal as he was lowering his boat lift into the water, watching the sun rising over the mangrove forest on the mainland side of the Matlacha river as the last of the night's mosquitoes bit his neck for a quick snack. He swatted them away and sprayed some bug repellent on his arms and neck. The growing sun and awful smell from the bug spray cleared the area of the nuisance.

One of the worst things about Florida was the mosquito. Lee County has its own mosquito control district to try to battle the pest. They have old DC-3's and Vietnam-era helicopters for spraying the insecticide fog over the swampy areas where the mosquitoes breed. The planes and helicopters formed the largest air force for insect control in the world. Doug thought of his rugged ancestors who had survived in Lee County before any mosquito control. They were truly a resourceful bunch and they enjoyed their farms and commercial fishing in paradise. One of Doug's great uncles said one time after getting caught in a traffic jam on U.S. 41 that he would rather have more mosquitoes than all of the Yankees and their real estate developers with their taxes funding mosquito control. Doug agreed that the price of progress was steep.

As usual Roger was late. From his boat, he could hear Roger's old Buick Regal before he turned into Doug's drive. The distinct sound of worn brakes broke the morning silence as Roger tried to make up for his lateness. After Roger had turned off the engine, the exhaust backfired and caused a great blue heron to let out a loud squawk and fly from his perch on Doug's roof.

Roger walked huffing into the back yard with his abundant belly bouncing and said, "Sorry I'm late. The traffic was backed up because of the road construction."

"No big deal. I've got the boat gassed up and ready to go. I've got a couple of fishing rods in case we need a break," Doug noted.

Roger handed his duffel bag filled with lunch, drinks and a camera to Doug and stepped into the *Two Tongues* as he said, "I haven't seen the boat since you had it refinished, repowered and renamed. How fast will it go?"

Doug loaded the supplies into his cooler and answered, "Loaded with fuel and water in the live well, it'll go about 55. Low fuel and no water in the well, it'll hit 60 with one person."

Roger untied the ropes and Doug eased the throttle into gear. The wake from the slowly moving boat slapped up against the seawall sending the small fidler crabs scurrying up above the barnacle line of high tide. As they entered the Matlacha River and idled to the main channel, a steady north wind sent a chill down Doug's spine as he said, "It's spring time. Why's it still so cold in the morning?"

Roger answered, "Oh, quit complaining. It's snowing up north and you complain when you have to wear a jacket in the mornings. There is one advantage to being fat; my walrus fat insulates me from the weather."

Doug laughed and shrugged his shoulders. Roger continued, "On the way to your house this morning I stopped at the *7-11* for coffee and a doughnut. I got behind this lady who was cashing a bunch of scratch off lottery tickets. Her and the clerk got into it over how much credit she got. I was getting mad, but I just turned around and looked at the people in line behind me.

"The man behind me was a young construction worker with a 12-pack of Budweiser and Marlboros, behind him a heavy middle-aged lady with a bag of small Snickers bars and the National Enquirer. Then it hit me. A better name than *7-11* would be *Habits-R-Us*.

"Everybody goes there for their habit fix. Me, I needed my caffeine, fat and sugar. The guy behind me alcohol and nicotine. The lady in the back required a sugar fix with her gossip. Think about it. *Habits-R-Us* is a better name, don't you think?"

Doug chuckled and replied, "I think you had too much coffee."

Roger was miffed but he continued, "And another thing that bothers me is how everybody is so forgiving about their own habits but judgmental about others. Think about it. The lady buying the Snickers looks at the construction worker and thinks, 'that poor addict is buying booze and cigarettes at eight in the morning.' The construction worker looks at the heavy lady and thinks, 'I can't believe someone that fat is buying candy to eat while reading her gossip rag.'"

Doug threw up his hands, "O.K., you win. From now on, I'll call all *7-11* stores *Habits-R-Us* if you promise to give me a little quiet this morning."

Roger smiled and finished drinking his coffee, as he silently vowed to change his own bad habits.

Roger changed the subject, "Well, I guess you heard Buck made bond yesterday."

Doug answered incredulously, "What? How in the world did he come up with $300,000 in collateral and $30,000 for a bondsman's fee? He's poor as dirt."

Roger said, "I think it confirms what we've thought all along. He did this with another person or persons. Someone strong enough to come up with that bond."

Roger and Doug were quiet as they racked their brains trying to think of Buck's conspirators. Once into the main channel,

Doug pushed the throttle down and the boat jumped up on plane. They cruised in silence at about 35 mph around the tip of Bokeelia into Pine Island Sound. It was high tide so they took the short cut between Cat Key and Josslyn Island. They slowed down and came off plane at Hemp Key as Doug said, "I need something to drink."

As Doug was drinking his soda, Roger asked, "Isn't this the island the divorce hole is around?"

Doug started laughing so hard he had to spit out his drink. "I was wondering if you'd recognize it. You were mad as hell the day we unloaded everything."

Five years before Roger had gone through a painful divorce from his first wife. They had been married three years and thankfully had no children. His ex-wife moved back to Indiana after the divorce and left their former home in shambles. Roger had to clean everything up to ready the house for sale. She had left old lamps, full cat litter boxes, broken cement blocks and a rusty patio set.

Roger asked Doug to help him move the junk with his pickup. After they finished loading everything in the pickup, Doug suggested that all of the junk might make a good artificial reef in one of his deep fishing holes. They loaded everything into Doug's boat, linking everything together with an old chain. When they dumped it overboard Roger let out a triumphant scream, and then he started crying. Doug opened two beers, gave one to his friend and headed back home with only the sound of the wind between them.

When they were idling back to Doug's dock, Roger broke the silence and said, "Well, at least ten years from now I can catch a fish out of the divorce hole and say I got something good from my first marriage."

Doug laughed as he realized his friend was on the painful road to recovery.

*   *   *   *

Doug and Roger finished their sodas while they continued their trip to the Roosevelt Channel behind Captiva Island. The first manatee was found drifting in the channel behind 'Tween Waters Inn. The second manatee was found at the mouth of McIntire Creek in Ding Darling Sanctuary. The third manatee, the baby, was found impaled on a mangrove branch next to the main road in Ding Darling Sanctuary that borders a wide bay. All of the manatees were beheaded. There were no clues to what happened to their heads. It was a bizarre mystery that the media seized on like rabid jackals.

As Roger was loading up his camera with fresh film he asked, "What's your take on Buck Williams? Does he have a pattern of violence?"

Doug laughed, "No, Buck is like most of the commercial fisherman around here. For generations their families have earned a living netting fish. When the net ban was passed, it put a lot of people out of business. Before the net ban they were a very independent sort. They didn't care about government as long as it didn't bother them.

"When the net ban put them out of business, some of 'em became very belligerent. They violated the new laws and if they got caught, they paid the fines. They considered it a price of doing business. Most of the other former netters started doing clam and scallop harvesting in made-made farms in Pine Island Sound. The State sanctioned it and gave them cheap leases of the submerged land. Now, the state comes in with these new slow zones and it triples the amount of time needed to harvest the seafood. As you can imagine, the commercial fishermen hate the increased government regulations.

"Buck was never a leader in the fight against more regulation. He just fished and tried to provide for his family. He always sort of stayed to himself. I just don't understand why he did this. The fishermen are a very proud people and they've been unfairly blamed for a lot of bad things the past few years. You know, every man has his breaking point."

21

After a few hours of taking pictures of the areas where the carcasses had been found, they took a break to have lunch and discuss trial strategy. After a working lunch while drifting in Doug's boat, they decided to treat themselves to some fishing around Demere Key. Doug started up the *Two Tongues* and drove across the intracoastal channel, around the clam farms south of Demere Key and came off plane in the channel in front of the island.

Doug turned off his engine and while he drifted towards the shallow water surrounding the island, he put down his trolling motor. He engaged the quiet trolling motor and headed towards one of his fishing holes in front of the main house on Demere Key.

Roger asked, "What is that house made of?"

Doug answered, "Well I've never been in it, but it looks like large shells cemented together."

Roger looked at the strange tan-colored house while rigging his rod with a root beer colored plastic grub inserted on a redhead colored jig. When he cast his jig towards the island, he saw some large birds walking down the hill towards the boat. The birds looked a bit like turkeys, but their feathers were different colors. All of a sudden they started letting out an obnoxiously loud squawk that put the blue heron to shame.

"What kind of birds are they? They hurt my ears," Roger complained.

"Peacocks. The owner has them on the island—they're very protective of their turf. They're telling us to kiss off," Doug explained.

Roger was watching the peacocks preen and spread their wings when his fishing rod was jerked from his hands and landed in the shallow water.

"I lost my rod. The fished yanked it from my hands," Roger yelled.

Doug turned on the trolling motor and followed the rod through the shallow grass flats. When they got in two feet of water they could see the rod slow down as it moved through the

22

turtle grass. Roger was embarrassed over loosing his rod and determined to make up for his clumsiness. He stepped to the tip of the bow and jumped towards his fleeing rod. His well-intentioned jump was more of a belly-buster than a strategic rescue attempt. Doug started laughing as Roger floundered about looking for his rod. He saw it a few feet ahead of him and pounced on it, holding on with all his strength. He stood up, sputtering the water from his mouth, and lifted the rod out of the water. The line on the reel started making a shrill sound as it stripped off the spool. Roger handed the rod to Doug, who had motored the boat over. Roger waded to the back of the boat and climbed in, exhausted from his flailing around.

"What are you waiting for? This is your fish, come fight him," Doug chided.

Roger groaned and walked to the bow, retrieving his well-traveled rod and reel. After a 10-minute battle, Doug netted Roger's 26-inch redfish and put him in the cooler. Roger grabbed a cold beer and relaxed after his unorthodox catch. It was Doug's turn and he caught and released two oversized redfish before he landed one that was the legal size. With their redfish on ice for dinner, they drove back to Matlacha as they silently pondered why someone would do such a horrible thing to a helpless manatee.

Chapter 6

George Steinworth IV founded *Save Our Seacows (SOS)* back in 1985 to promote the preservation of the seacow, also called a manatee. Steinworth was a trust fund baby who grew up on exclusive Sanibel Island. During his 63 years of privilege on Sanibel, he had seen the population explosion and the changes it caused on the island. When he was a child, he was able to paddle his canoe from his family home on the shores of Tarpon Bay across Pine Island Sound without seeing more than a dozen boats on any given day.

He saw how mercury contamination of the early 1970's almost wiped out the osprey population. He had joined a local committee that traveled to Tallahassee and lobbied the state legislature in 1971 for changes in pollution control. His lobbying efforts were successful and new laws were passed restricting pollution. He watched with delight how the osprey returned to a healthy population in the late '70s. Every time he paddled his canoe through Pine Island Sound, he watched with awe as the majestic bird stalked its prey from hundreds of feet above the fish before diving into the water with its talons extended and flying away with lunch.

The osprey continued their return to a healthy population and adapted to man's intrusion into their environment. By 2000, almost every channel marker in Pine Island Sound had an osprey's nest located on top of the pole, wedged between the painted markers. Every time Steinworth drove off Sanibel, he would be delighted with seeing the osprey nests built on the highest trees overlooking Summerlin Boulevard and the mangrove forests that bordered it. The power company tried to provide the osprey with platforms for their nests to offer it choices other than their power poles. These ready-made nesting platforms were made with standard wooden power poles and a metal grate at the top about 4 foot square.

Steinworth had watched one of these ready-made nests inhabited by an osprey family over the years. It was about a mile from the Sanibel Causeway on the south side of Summerlin near the McGregor Boulevard turnoff. A pair of ospreys occupied this nest and raised different generations over the years while watching 5,000 cars a day drive under them less than 100 feet away. Ospreys had adapted and with reasonable protection laws had prospered.

One spring day in 1985, Steinworth was paddling his canoe in Tarpon Bay and a fishing boat blew by at high speed. As he was turning his canoe into the oncoming wake, a manatee, swimming away from the noisy boat, surfaced next to his canoe. The nostril blow frightened Steinworth, but the manatee hadn't heard the canoe and was surprised when he saw it in his path. The manatee quickly dove and its tail flume hit Steinworth's canoe and tipped him over. As Steinworth climbed back into his canoe, he decided it was time to promote slow speed zones for manatees.

Steinworth founded *Save Our Seacows* and used the acronym of *SOS* on T-shirts and bumper stickers to promote the club. Over the years, environmentalists and politicians backed *SOS* because the gentle giant was so warm and huggable. All of the political focus groups said voters supported anything that was pro-manatee. *SOS* grew over the years and by the turn of the century had over a million members worldwide. They had biologists and lawyers on their staff full-time to promote manatee protection measures. Because of manatee slow zones and boater awareness, the manatee population started to grow in the early 1990's and by 2000 there were so many manatees they were considered being taken off the endangered species list. Like the osprey, reasonable government regulations had helped the manatee adapt to the human population encroaching into their environment.

*   *   *   *

Steve Saylor founded *Save Our Speed (SOS)* in 1999 to try to fight the growing manatee regulations. The original manatee regulations in the late '80s had made sense to Steve. The Caloosahatchee River was a deep river that flowed from Lake Okeechobee into the Gulf of Mexico at the base of the Sanibel Causeway. Thirty miles up river from the mouth of the Caloosahatchee, the smaller Orange River flowed into the Caloosahatchee where I-75 crossed the river. The power company had a plant between the two rivers that pulled brackish water in from the Caloosahatchee and cooled the massive generators that produced electricity and discharged the heated water into the Orange River, which flowed down a curving path into the Caloosahatchee.

This heated water provided a winter sanctuary for the warm-blooded manatees, and they congregated around the power plant when the temperature dropped. The original manatee regulations required boats go slow in this area during the cold months. Steve and most boaters agreed this was a reasonable regulation to protect the manatee.

The second level of manatee protection came a few years later. The manatees traveled to the power plant in the fall and left sometime in the spring to head to the open Gulf. During their leisurely travels up and down the river, they stopped in canals, creeks and lagoons. The manatees eat seagrass in the shallow areas of the river nearer the shore. Because of this pattern, the next manatee regulation was that all boats in canals, creeks and within quarter mile of the shore had to go slow. This increased regulation met with some resistance but was accepted by Steve and the majority of boaters because there were valid reasons for it.

In the early 80's, it was an event to see a manatee swim past while you were fishing. Steve and his friends noticed the manatee population increasing during the 90's. By 2000 you usually saw five or six per fishing trip. The manatee population was increasing, along with the number of manatee deaths.

Steve Saylor was a lawyer and native of Ft. Myers. One of his clients, a rich developer of waterfront condos, hired him in 1995 to help him get permits for one of his new projects on the Caloosahatchee River. The following two years of legal battles were a quick education in the murky area of waterfront development and manatee regulations.

The statistics compiled by the state and research funded privately by the power company were seemingly straightforward. The four leading areas of manatee deaths in the Caloosahatchee were (1) old age and other natural causes, such as red tide and cold stress, (2) collisions with power boats with outboard engines, (3) accidents at locks on the river and canals that opened and shut based on flood control, and (4) collisions with barges and large yachts.

'Collisions with barges and large yachts' held a particular interest for the power company. The power company had two barges that traveled up and down the Caloosahatchee to the port of Boca Grande twice a day bringing oil to the power plant to burn and convert to electricity. They didn't want the public relations nightmare of being blamed for an excessive number of manatee deaths because their barges ran them over on a regular basis. During Steve's research, he discovered that the power company gave large monetary grants to the researcher who authored the studies. He thought it was an amazing coincidence that all of the studies said the barges were only a "minimal" cause of manatee deaths.

During the permitting process, Steve took a deposition of a veterinarian that performed manatee necropsies for the state to determine cause of death. During the deposition, Steve discovered that many of the dead manatees floating in the river had prop scars on their back because their carcasess were run over after death. A manatee could have died a natural death and been floating in the channel at night when hit by a boater, leaving prop scars. However, the government policy was to list any dead manatee with prop scars as "caused by boaters."

The veterinarian also noted that many of the manatees had massive internal injuries that could not have been caused by a single collision with a boat. The vet's opinion was that a large yacht or barge killed the manatee with a collision and the floating carcass was later run over by a small boat, leaving prop scars. However, the government policy was to list the cause of death as "caused by boaters."

Steve discovered that a lot of groups with selfish agendas supported the increased manatee regulations. All of the anti-growth groups supported the manatee regulations because it made Florida less attractive to boaters. The anti-growth groups weren't able to get building moratoriums passed but achieved the same result by supporting the warm and huggable manatee that was so popular with politicians and musicians.

In 1999, Steve became outraged with the new manatee proposals for the Caloosahatchee River, Matlacha River and Pine Island Sound. The proposals called for slow speed in 70% of the area and a 25-mph speed zone in the remaining area. He formed *Save Our Speed (SOS)* and started to recruit members and sponsors. His first recruit was his life-long friend, Mark Shaw.

Mark was a banker who fished more than he worked. Actually, his fishing was an important business development area for the bank. Current and future clients were treated to fishing trips to insure their loyalty to the bank. Mark did more business in his boat than any of his competitors ever did on golf courses. Mark's favorite saying was "Golf is my favorite sport—it keeps people off the water while I'm fishing."

Mark was on his third wife, but she was his first trophy wife. His first wife was his high school sweetheart and they had three children together. His first wife found out about his weekly drunken forays to the strip clubs and divorced him. His child support for three children quickly drained him, and he began dating rich divorcees. He finally convinced one to marry him, and he did a good enough job of co-mingling her money in their bank accounts that he was able to have a nice nest egg when he divorced her eight years later. Mark was 58 and kept himself in shape by riding his bike after work. His trophy wife was 32 and worked at a health club. Mark felt he had finally succeeded whenever he went boating with his trophy wife, proudly displayed in a thong bikini. All of Mark's fishing buddies admired his first mate.

One month after *Save Our Speed* was founded, *Save Our Seacows* sued them for trademark infringement over the acronym *SOS* in their advertising. Six months of litigation and $30,000 in legal fees later, *Save Our Speed* was successful in getting the suit thrown out. *Save Our Seacows* had successfully tied up their time and resources responding to their frivolous lawsuit.

Save Our Seacows threw the gantlet down in front of Steve Saylor and Mark Shaw. Their professional appearances hid their extreme outrage toward the growing government interference in their way of life. Steve, Mark and their friends were not going to be defeated by carpetbaggers, tree huggers, and Sanibel trust fund babies. The war had just begun.

Save Our Speed filed a lawsuit against the state alleging the manatee laws were unconstitutional. They also researched the tax-exempt status of *Save Our Seacows* and discovered it was listed as a tax-exempt corporation. One of the conditions of their tax-exempt status was that they couldn't involve themselves in political lobbying. *Save Our Speed* filed a petition with the IRS to have the tax-exempt status taken away from them because of alleged lobbying. The depositions and paperwork kept two lawyers busy from each organization defending their positions.

The third plan of attack was to file personal injury lawsuits against the state because of boaters being injured running into the new unmarked manatee zone signs. The state and U.S. coast guard had an ongoing battle regarding reflective strips and lights on the new manatee signs. The coast guard claimed the signs couldn't be marked because the proper procedures weren't followed in the federal agencies. The state claimed they were state waters and they could do whatever they wanted.

Meanwhile, the signs remained unmarked and collisions continued to occur at an alarming rate. The crafty lawyers for

Save Our Speed sued both the state and federal government claiming that both were negligent. This created a classic conflict that had the two governments counter-suing and cross-suing each other. It also produced a paper war with all of the different motions and legal papers filed by each side.

Save Our Seacows didn't sit around and watch the parties fight without them; they petitioned the court to allow them to intervene to supposedly represent the manatees. Both *Save Our Seacows* and *Save Our Speed* raised over $500,000 to fight the different lawsuits. Neither side was backing down with their legal pleadings and each side was manipulating the court of public opinion.

Chapter 7

"I wish I had more witnesses to the actual killing of the manatees," Roger lamented to Doug.

They had spent the afternoon in Roger's office going over all of the witness statements and reports of experts. Roger wanted more evidence about who was involved in the killings besides Buck. It was obvious that this was not a one-man job.

Doug said, "We know whoever is helping Buck has some money. I'm also sure Buck is not the brains behind the killings. Who would profit from a dead manatee? It's been three weeks since the killings and we still don't know why."

After about five seconds of silence, Roger spoke up, "Why don't you go out to your old stomping grounds and see what people on the island are saying. I also need to know what Dr. Jones can testify to at trial. I'll have my secretary see if he's available this afternoon."

Roger buzzed his secretary and requested she schedule the meeting. Doug walked over to the wall with the map of Pine Island Sound taped on and thought about the unknown capture points. Doug's concentration was interrupted as Roger's secretary buzzed back with the news Dr. Jones was available in his Naples office for a late afternoon conference. Doug told her he was available and to confirm a four o'clock meeting time.

Roger said, "Dr. Jones has been doing necropsy work for us for the past ten years. He knows his stuff and he'll tell you what he thinks about a death. He doesn't care if it matches your theory of the case or not. More often than not, the defense lawyers use his report against us at trial. Ask him about anything unusual because I'm sure he has an opinion about it."

Doug answered, "I understand. I'll go on a fishing expedition with him. I'm going to head on down there; with tourist traffic it's a two hour drive."

During the drive down to Naples, Doug turned on his favorite country music station and thought about the case. How did Buck capture two adult manatees and a baby in one night? How did he keep the manatees in place so he could kill them with the chain saw? Were they already dead when he cut off their heads? The questions went unanswered as Doug avoided the bad drivers drifting with the sea of traffic, flowing south towards Naples.

At 4:05 p.m. Doug pulled his old Ford truck into the parking lot. Doug was irritable after fighting the traffic all of the way. As he walked into Dr. Jones waiting room, he realized the doctor was also running late. Doug let the receptionist know he had arrived and then walked over to the magazine rack. After a quick survey, he settled on the latest issue of *Cosmopolitan*. He enjoyed reading women's magazines because it educated him on the feminine thought process. Some of his best lines over the years he had stolen from *Cosmopolitan's* advice page.

After twenty minutes of reading, a grandfatherly figure opened the door and said, "Hello, Detective Shearer. I'm Dr. Jones, pleased to meet you."

After the pair shook hands, Doug followed the doctor back to his office. It was a small, windowless office with the obligatory diplomas hanging from the cream colored walls. Dr. Jones desk was covered with papers, medical journals and old coffee cups.

"Have a seat, detective. What can I do for you?"

"I've got some questions about the headless manatees. The person we caught with one of the manatees has pled not guilty to harassment of the manatees and we've got to prove the manatee was trapped or killed by this person. I was wondering if there is any information you could give me to help us figure this out?"

"The manatees were beheaded very near the time of death. However, I think they were already dead, or at least tranquilized or subdued when the heads were cut off. The reason for this is that the cuts were straight. If the manatee was still moving, there would have been jagged cuts from the chainsaw."

Doug nodded and Dr. Jones continued after a deep breath, "We also found some fiberglass shards on the left side of the two adult manatees. I'm not sure what it means, but I've sent them out for analysis. Other than that, nothing was unusual about the animals."

Doug hesitated and then asked, "Dr. Jones, I don't want you to take this the wrong way, but how many necropsies have you done on manatees?"

Dr. Jones laughed and said, "I'm not sure exactly. But at least 100; which is more than any other veterinarian in the state has done. Let me explain what I mean. The state claims that they have done hundreds of necropsies on dead manatees. But to have a true, scientific necropsy, a licensed veterinarian that has been trained is the only person that should be doing a necropsy.

"If you remember, a few years ago we had a bad outbreak of red tide and a lot of manatees died. The state hired biologist and students to do these necropsies. They had no idea what they were doing. So they developed a generic buzzword they called 'cold stress.'

"Well, let me tell you what some of the state's biologist have lumped under 'cold stress' as the cause of death. Two years ago, down in the Ten Thousand Islands, some government workers thought it would help the water flow in a canal to kill off all of the hydrilla plants. They do this in December—just as all of the manatees are migrating up the rivers and canals to try to stay warm during the winter. The hydrilla plants were what they normally ate in the brackish water.

"There was this one five-foot long manatee that died with dirt in his stomach. The manatee only weighed ninety pounds. A healthy manatee that length would weigh three times that amount. I concluded that the animal died of starvation because it was so skinny and there was not a lot of food in the canal. The dirt at the bottom of the canal was the closest thing that smelled like hydrilla, so the manatee ate the dirt. The state's biologist labeled the death 'cold strees.'"

Doug asked, "Why would they do that?"

Dr. Jones replied, "There's a big controversy about the manatee and all the slow zones. The state's biologist are biased because any manatee death that they can't trace to boat collisions, they label 'cold stress' to avoid any further investigation that might embarrass them or hurt their agenda. I'll give you another example. A high number of baby manatees die every year. The state biologist claim they don't know why, so they label the deaths 'cold stress.' The truth is that the baby manatees die because they follow their mothers up river to these man-made warm water sanctuaries caused by the outflow from power plants. The problem is that there is not enough food for the manatees. The adult manatees are seen every year lifting their heads into the air to eat vegetation hanging over creeks and rivers. The baby manatees can't reach the food. When the mother manatees head back down river, the babies don't have the energy to survive.

"However, the power companies donate hundreds of thousands of dollars to manatee preservation and they allow groups to construct observation decks next to the canals at the plants. The truth is that these baby manatees are being systematically starved to death. 'Cold stress' is a lot better sounding than 'starvation.'

Doug asked, "What would you do different to help save the manatee from more deaths?"

Dr. Jones was on a roll. His face was red and small beads of perspiration had formed on his forehead as he continued, "First of all, the whole concentration of government is misplaced. The studies show that the boater is responsible for 25% of the manatee deaths. I think that's a high number, but for argument's sake let's assume that to be true. Why doesn't government look at the other 75% of deaths? I'll tell you why—they can't handle the truth. The artificial warm water sanctuaries created by power plants have altered the winter migration of the species. Instead of swimming south to the Everglades, the keys or the Caribbean for the winter, the lazy animals are taking a shortcut to the warm water sanctuaries. The problem is they are not safe for the animals. All of the animals are packed into canal systems or rivers with very little food.

"All of the manatees produce a huge amount of waste from eating seagrass or whatever vegetation is available. Remember, these are seacows. This discharge smells up the area and is unsanitary. Imagine a seacow living in a sewer plant, but he lifts his head out of the water to eat plants that are living on the edge. That is what is happening in a lot of the winter areas.

"If the government really wanted to help the manatee, they would shut down theses artificial warm water areas. The manatee would relearn the historical migration routes and the species would prosper even more that it has."

After listening to Dr. Jones explain his theories, Doug was certain he would be a good witness at trial.

Chapter 8

Doug woke up to his neighbors across the canal trying to start the ancient outboard engine on their old 37-foot sailboat. The engine kept turning over slower and slower without catching. In the eight years Doug had lived on the canal he had only seen the sailboat moved twice. He put on shorts and a T-shirt and stumbled out to his driveway to get his morning paper. After he put the coffee on, he walked to his family room window and looked across the canal to the faded, gray sailboat optimistically named *Athena*.

There was black smoke rising out of *Athena's* exhaust holes. The noise from the old engine became quieter as the battery lost its power. Doug walked outside and was greeted by a cloudy sunrise and a stiff northeast breeze. As he walked to the edge of his seawall, he could see the husband's shadow through the dusty window, below deck, furiously trying to start the engine as it started making the tell-tale clicking sound of a dead battery.

He heard the shrill voice of his neighbor's wife as she said, "Herb, my sister's flight will be here tonight. I told her we would go to Cabbage Key for lunch tomorrow. The boat will be ready, won't it?"

Doug could tell that this was not going to be a pleasant conversation so he quietly went back inside to get a cup of coffee and read the paper. As he expected, the front page had a lead story about the dead manatees. There were all sorts of wild speculation about who was behind the killings and why. It was great fodder for the news jackals and made great headlines. By this time, everyone in law enforcement and the media had figured out that Buck Williams couldn't have done all of this destruction by himself. Doug quickly scanned the articles for any information about the case that he didn't already know.

He then read the sports page, temporarily forgetting about the manatee case. After he had devoured the morning paper, he checked his e-mail for messages. His supervisor at the sheriff's office and Roger from the State Attorney's Office kept him updated on the progress of the manatee case. With nothing new in the investigation, he decided to get his daily workout completed. Doug remembered it was a swimming day as he glanced outside to the overcast sky. He could hear his neighbors arguing about who was responsible for the lack of maitenance and frozen engine on their sailboat.

Doug changed into his swimsuit and walked down to his dock. He kept a twelve foot aluminum ladder lying on the top of his seawall to avoid barnacles attaching themselves to the steps and cutting his feet. He picked it up and slid it into the water approximately four feet before it hit bottom. He twisted it from side to side to make sure it was sunk into the soft sand before leaning it against the seawall. The cool breeze made goose bumps appear all over Doug's body and he debated with himself about the sensibility of swimming in March. Doug quickly ended his internal debate by diving into the dark waters, as his neighbors temporarily stopped the blame game to gape at their odd neighbor.

The water was thankfully warmer than the air, and Doug quickly surfaced and swam down the canal towards the mouth. He was at the west end of his canal, which was a quarter mile long. It opened to the east and emptied into the Matlacha River about one half-mile north of the Matlacha bridge. Doug's workout was to swim to the mouth of the canal and return. Other than the occasional boater coming or going down the canal, it was usually a straight swim as he alternated with different strokes.

After Doug started his return, he switched to the backstroke. About a minute into his return trip, his right shoulder blade received a forceful bump. Doug was startled and stopped swimming, allowing his legs to come underneath him. He had an uneasy feeling as he looked around the tannin-stained water and saw nothing. He felt another forceful bump in his chest, and he brought his arms up in front of his face. The water sprayed into his face as he felt the creature come out of the water while still touching his chest. The adrenaline shot through his body as he wiped the water off his eyes to see what was attacking him. He focused and realized he was staring into the dark eyes of a manatee with a head twice as big as his, less than a foot away. The manatee looked at him and slowly moved its mouth towards Doug, almost as if trying to kiss him. Doug was amused until he smelled the bad breath of the large mammal while treading water.

Doug relaxed as he realized the manatee was just curious. Doug treaded water for a few minutes as the manatee swam around him, slowly brushing against him. Doug continued back to his dock as the manatee swam about 10 yards behind him. All of his neighbors were delighted as he led the manatee parade up his canal. When Doug was in front of his house, he treaded water and waited to see what the gentle mammal would do next. The manatee swam next to him and poked his head towards him while blowing out air, sending a slight mist across his face. Doug reached out and petted the manatee behind the ears. He was pleasantly surprised when the manatee leaned his head towards Doug's hand like a dog would if he wanted more. After a few seconds of petting his new friend, Doug climbed up his ladder and pulled it in behind him. He watched the manatee as it slowly swam back towards the mouth of his canal.

Doug went inside and showered, his thoughts returning to the manatee investigation. He was meeting Big Papa for lunch at the *Lazy Flamingo* restaurant on Bokeelia. Big Papa and Buck Williams had grown up together on Pine Island, and Doug wanted to find out if Big Papa would have any idea why Buck or his unknown co-conspirators would kill three manatees.

As Doug drove to the *Lazy Flamingo*, he remembered the first time he met Big Papa. Doug's college roommate and football teammate at Florida State was Sandy Harper, Big Papa's son. Sandy had invited Doug to his house for spring break during their junior year. They drove down from Tallahassee in Doug's old Ford pickup and arrived right at sunset. There was a crushed shell and sand drive at the end of the last paved road at Bokeelia, on the north end of Pine Island. Big Papa had painted an oversized sign warning of *Bad Dogs* next to the mailbox that greeted any potential visitor. As Doug parked his Ford under an oak tree, an old black Labrador retriever greeted them.

Sandy jumped out and called, "Come here, Hannah. I missed my girl."

Doug watched as the black lab ran over, licked Sandy and yelped with excitement. Hannah then came over and licked Doug just like he was family. When Doug looked up, he saw Big Papa coming out of the old wooden house. Big Papa was a stout man with a receding hairline but powerful shoulders, forearms and hands. A lifetime of commercial fishing showed on his tanned, weathered face, but his dark blue eyes and warm smile made Doug feel comfortable. Big Papa had an old Coleman lantern lit and hanging from the lowest branch on the oak tree next to a wooden picnic table.

Sandy walked over, hugged his Dad and said, "Daddy, this is my roomie I've told you about, Doug."

Big Papa walked over to Doug, shook his hand and said, "Son, it's nice to meet ya; Sandy's told me a lot about ya. Just call me Big Papa. You boys ready for a cold beer?"

Doug and Sandy gladly accepted as Big Papa opened up the cooler on top of the picnic table and tossed them a beer. They sat down around the picnic table telling college stories and jokes until midnight. As the conversation was slowing down, a red convertible mustang pulled into the drive with rock music blaring. As the dust settled, the passenger door opened and the most gorgeous blonde Doug had ever seen slid out of the seat and waved goodbye to her girlfriend. She walked over and hugged Sandy while Doug's eyes admired the womanly curves on the tan young goddess dressed out in a black leather miniskirt and red half-shirt.

Sandy said, "Doug, this is my jailbait sister, Amanda."

Big Papa laughed as Amanda playfully slapped Sandy. Doug blushed and offered his handshake while saying, "My name's Doug; it's nice to meet you Amanda."

Amanda shook his hand, holding it longer than appropriate while smiling at Doug. She finally said, "I'll only be jailbait for another year. If you're a starter on the football team by then, maybe we can talk."

Doug vividly remembered the day he met the love of his life.

Doug had to drag himself from memory lane as he parked his old Ford at the *Lazy Flamingo*. He went inside and saw Big Papa sitting at the bar drinking a draft beer.

Big Papa said loudly across the restaurant, "Doug, come on over. I was just havin' my favorite appetizer while I was waiting on ya."

Doug shook his hand, sat down and said, "It's good to see ya, Big Papa. You're looking good."

"Well, for an old man, I'm doing all right. You don't look so good; got bags under your eyes."

"These manatee killings with Buck Williams has got me working overtime. Lot of pressure from up top. Know what I mean?"

Big Papa nodded and said, "Yeah, I bet. It's all over the news. But I don't care how busy you are, ya still gotta eat. The graveyard is filled with irreplaceable people. You take a break and let's get a mess of stone crab claws with some clam chowder; it'll put some meat on your bones. After lunch we'll talk about Buck."

Doug agreed and they placed their order and talked about the local gossip and the latest fishing news until lunch came. After a fantastic lunch, Doug decided it was time to get down to business.

He looked at Big Papa and said quietly, "I know you're friends with Buck. What's going on with him? He hasn't been the same since his wife died last year."

Big Papa shifted on his barstool, took a drink of his beer and slowly replied, "I'm not sure what's gotten into 'em. We used to go huntin' and fishin' together but since his wife died, he just stays around the house. Sometimes, I'll see him with his grandsons at the grocery store, they're five and three now. His daughter, Baylee, is sweet as ever, but that no-good husband of 'ers is back in jail for his third DUI. You know his son, Carl; he's married but his wife had a miscarriage a few months back. Outside of his family, I think Buck just don't care no more."

Doug nodded and debated what to say for a few seconds, "Well a lot of people want his hide. All of the politicians want to hang him and that *Save Our Seacows* club has told the press that he should get life in prison for this."

Big Papa sat straight up and raised his voice, "Those politicians ain't good for nothin'—they're too scared to steal and too lazy to work. I saw that interview with the president of that manatee club, George Steinworth. That son-of-a-bitch used to charter Buck to take 'im tarpon fishin' and now he's talkin' about putting 'im in prison for life. I guess we know what kind of friend he is."

Doug smiled as he thought about leaking that information to some of the bulldog newspaper reporters. It would be fun to watch Steinworth squirm, but Doug thought better of it.

Big Papa continued, "I wonder why he had to chop off their heads; sounds like some damn heathen. I will tell you something, though. The commercial fishermen are pissed off at all of this government regulation. First, the net ban. Now, the slow zones are costing them more money. Yes sir, they are pissed off at all the bureaucrats."

Doug asked, "Do you think any of the commercial guys are behind this besides Buck? There's no way he could do all this himself."

Big Papa scratched his chin while considering his answer, "I know there's no way Buck is in this by himself. He ain't strong enough or smart enough to pull this off. You know I normally hear talk on the island whenever somethin' is going on. But I ain't heard nothing about these dead manatees."

41

Doug paid the tab, and they walked out to Doug's truck. The clouds had cleared and the sun was bearing down on them as they talked about going snook fishing. As they were shaking hands and saying goodbye, Big Papa said, "I almost forgot something, Doug. Amanda's divorce was final last week and she moved back into town, over in some fancy Cape Coral condo on the river. She told me to have you call her."

Doug's hair on the back of his neck stiffened and his face flushed as he became light-headed. He definitely did not have time for Amanda. After a few seconds, Doug smiled meekly and asked Big Papa, "What's her number?"

Chapter 9

Doug's anxiety was multiplying exponentially as he drove in to the entrance of Amanda' new riverfront condo. Amanda's address was the newest high-rise built on the Cape Coral side of the Caloosahatchee River. A visitor was required to drive in the closest lane to the guardhouse so the attendant could buzz the residence to see if the lord or lady of the manor would receive a common guest. After Doug was waived through to the guest parking area, he was directed to the elevator where he punched 18, the penthouse level.

As Doug's mind raced on the slow rise to luxury, he thought of his prior courtship of Ms. Amanda Harper. After the first spring break at his roommate's house on Bokeelia, Doug tried to forget his roommate's gorgeous jailbait sister. Amanda was determined not to let this happen; she loved to call and leave descriptive messages on Doug's answering machine at Florida State describing how she felt when thinking of him. When Amanda called and caught Doug at home, they would have long talks. Doug was so concerned about Amanda turning 18 and his lustful thoughts, he decided to spend his next spring break in Key West.

After spring break, he returned to Tallahassee and, thankfully, no messages on his answering machine from Amanda. The following Friday night after returning from spring break, he came back to his dorm room after a night out with the guys. When he opened the door and turned on the overhead light, he saw Amanda's head sticking out of the covers from his bed.

He quickly shut his door and said, "What are you doing here? Sandy could come in at any time!"

Amanda purred, "Oh don't worry about it, choir boy. I talked to his girlfriend earlier this week, and I've got it covered.

43

He's staying at her place tonight and I'm staying here—if that's O.K. with you"

When Amanda pulled the sheets off of her naked, lubricious body proudly displayed in the bright light, Doug's throat went dry and his head started to spin. Doug was transfixed by Amanda's shapely body, which was tanned the color of weathered cypress wood, except for a freckle line above her milky white breasts that defied gravity. The last thing he remembered was locking the door before consuming the apples of his own Garden of Eden.

After their love affair was officially consummated, Doug could not think of another woman. He would finish his classes on a Friday and drive down to Bokelia to spend the weekend with Amanda. After Doug graduated from Florida State with his criminology degree, he moved back to Ft. Myers and started work with the Lee County Sheriff's Office. He was 22 and full of unbridled optimism while Amanda was an eighteen-year-old beauty who wanted her own house. Doug and Amanda moved in together and were a happy couple until she turned 26 and realized that Doug was never going to be able to buy her a beachfront mansion with a cop's salary.

Amanda could not face Doug and tell him her reasons for leaving. She had just left a note on their bed, written in red ink.

Dear Dougie,

We had some great times together and I will always love you. But I want something more than being a cop's wife in little old Ft. Myers. You'll make someone a great husband. I wish you the best.

Love always, Amanda

Amanda moved to Sarasota and married a rich real estate developer within the year. It had been four years since Amanda had left, and Doug was still infatuated with her. He had dated different women but none had opened up his heart since Amanda.

Doug was currently dating Mary White, a schoolteacher at the local high school. They had met about a year before, after her divorce, and had a casual relationship since. Lately, Mary had been complaining that Doug was fishing too much in his spare time.

The elevator rang quietly and alerted Doug that he was on the 18th floor. He walked off the elevator to an open air landing area that had a breeze blowing in from the river. On one side of the building Doug could see the river and on the other urban sprawl. He stepped to the only door in sight and rang Amanda's doorbell. After a long pause, the door opened and Amanda stood in the doorway dressed in a white terry cloth robe with a towel wrapped around her wet hair.

"Oh, Dougie, it's so good to see you. Come in and give me a hug."

Doug looked at a freshly showered Amanda and his heart rate doubled as she stepped forward and pulled him into a strong hug. He gripped her and returned her squeeze. The smell of her freshly scrubbed body immediately brought back memories of passionate nights with little sleep.

Amanda smiled wistfully and invited him into her den. She pulled out a faded piece of light green stationary from her armoire and handed it to Doug who was sitting in her red velvet Queen Anne chair. She drifted behind Doug and began gently massaging his shoulders. He instantly recognized the paper and how he had bared his innermost feelings to Amanda so many years ago. As he touched the paper and began to read his words to the only poem he had ever written, the old wounds in his hardened heart ripped open even more painfully than the first time. He had to take a deep breath before he started to read his long ago thoughts, typed with an old typewriter, on the only stationary he had ever bought.

The Couple

They looked across the water at the setting sun.
She admired the fading colors as others had done.
She felt secure and enjoyed the blue jays' harmony.
She knew tomorrow would be another day of serenity.

He saw the small cloud above the red.
It was part of the picture, yet it was dead.
The happy colors changed from orange to blue to black.
He and the cloud knew what they so painfully lacked.

Amanda continued to massage his shoulders as he relaxed in the comfortable chair. As he felt his trapezoid muscles softening, he looked down to his left and saw Amanda's foot, perfectly tanned with red nail polish. He thought of the old debate from college about marriage—*"Was it better to marry someone that loved you more than you loved them, or vice versa?"*

In most of Doug's relationships he had been the one that was loved more. With Amanda he was on the other end of the equation, and they both knew it. Amanda pulled herself close to Doug's right ear, ran her hands through his hair and whispered to Doug, "Honey, that is the sweetest thing that anyone has ever done for me. Every time I showed that to my girlfriends they would cry."

"You did what?" Doug roared. "You showed my poem to other people?"

"Of course, honey. I wanted them to know how much you loved me. I thought it was cute," Amanda said while massaging Doug's biceps. As Doug steamed over his perceived betrayal, Amanda moved her head to the back of Doug's neck and gave him wet kisses on his neck and ears until Doug became dizzy with pleasure. He turned around and stared into Amanda's turquoise blue eyes as he surrendered his anger to the growing pleasure flowing through his body. Doug hated it when the logical part of his brain surrendered to Amanda's strong mating scent. As their lips locked, Doug promised himself that this was the last time he would let Amanda seduce him. And he meant it this time.

Chapter 10

Roger's nightmare was always the same. He's playing intramural flag football against his college fraternity's archrival team. His quarterback throws the ball up for grabs as time runs out and his team is down by two points. Roger is in the end zone and the ball is coming towards him. He can hear the footsteps of defenders as he jumps for the ball. As Roger reaches for the football, a pair of hands reaches over his back and grabs the ball as he falls to the ground. When Roger looks up he sees his elementary school bully, Bobby Earlich, laughing at him holding the football. Bobby says, "If you weren't so fat you could have jumped higher and gotten the ball."

Roger looks around and sees his little league coach and his high school gym teacher on the sideline shaking their heads in disappointment. Behind them, he sees his 8th grade girlfriend and she yells, "I told you to eat a salad."

Roger looks on the other side of the field and he sees his first wife. She looks at him, shrugs her shoulders, turns around and walks away. Roger runs after her as it starts to rain. He yells for her to wait as she keeps walking away. The rain gets harder and harder as he loses sight of her and then lightening flashes and thunder explodes. Roger always wakes up at this point in his nightmare, appropriately wet with sweat.

Roger had been born heavy and he had stayed that way while growing up. Little League was the only organized sport he ever participated in as a child. In college, Roger decided he was tired of being fat and began a workout plan. He jogged and played basketball daily. When he graduated from college, he was in the best shape of his life. He felt empowered that he had transformed his soft, undisciplined body into that of a normal, active 22-year old college graduate.

Roger's weight had fluctuated since college. He kept colored tags, based on his weight, sewn on the inside of his suit pants; green for 220—240 pounds, yellow for 240—270, and his current tag of red, 270—300. It had been four years since Roger had worn his green-tagged suits. Every night before Roger went to sleep he imagined himself wearing his green-tagged suits. All of the self-help books had instructed him to envision himself in his desired condition immediately before sleep. He read most of these books while eating ice cream at night.

Roger's intellect was superior and his common sense was above average. This combination allowed him to communicate complicated legal theories to juries in simple words they understood. He also was able to do this without the jurors feeling he was talking down to them. He had a great talent for trial work, and he knew it. He also knew that he couldn't control his weight, except for that golden period during college when he had mastered his demons.

During Roger's college years he had eaten healthy and exercised two hours a day. His body responded enthusiastically, and he became more confident with his newly toned self. The college girls noticed Roger's newfound physique, and they enjoyed Roger's body also. This increased attention by the better-looking girls was intoxicating. Roger truly enjoyed the college learning experience.

After college, Roger entered law school at 180 pounds full of confidence and swagger. It lasted a day. The superior-acting professors and smart, aggressive students caused Roger to doubt his academic abilities for the first time in his life. Roger's workouts were less frequent and not nearly as intense. He found out the quick high from happy hour was better than the sweaty high from exercise. After three years of law school, Roger had put on forty pounds and gotten out of his daily exercise habit.

Roger became a prosecutor in the Ft. Myers division of the State Attorney's Office after law school. He had been there for the past 15 years and was considered the best trial attorney. All of the high profile, media intensive cases went to him. His 95% conviction rate had made his boss look damn good over the years.

*   *   *   *

Roger felt his heart thumping in his throat and his blood pressure rising even though he had three valiums in his system. "*You don't really need Lasik eye surgery*," he heard his right brain arguing. His left brain was telling him to calm down and that it was a safe elective surgery to cure his eyesight. Roger had worn glasses and/or contacts since he was nine years old and he had tired of the inconvenience. His right brain was convincing him that the risk of the surgery out-weighed the benefits. Roger got up out of his chair and walked to the door to make a fast get away when the nurse walked in the door.

The nurse smiled and said, "The doctor is ready Mr. Barklett. Your new vision is minutes away; please follow me."

Roger was too embarrassed to run away from the confident nurse, and he started thinking about his *new vision*. He slowly entered the bright room behind the nurse and saw two men dressed in green surgical scrubs standing behind the laser. The laser was about six-foot square with a long extension arm coming out of the top and angled toward the small operating table with fresh sheets. It reminded him of an oversized dentist's machine. Roger was guided towards the operating table and told to get on and lay down. Roger was just under 300 pounds and he had a quick nightmare about the table collapsing in the middle of surgery and one of his eyes being sliced open by the laser. Roger was pleasantly surprised that the small table was sturdy as he shifted his beefy frame to the middle of the table as precisely instructed by the nurse.

The nurse held her hands gently under Roger's head and said, "Lift up your head so I can position this stabilizing pillow under it."

Roger complied and asked, "What's this for?"

The nurse patiently explained, "We use the pillow to secure your head during the procedure. It is extremely important that your head doesn't move during the process."

She then put numbing drops in his eyes and told him to relax. As the pillow was positioned, the doctor walked around the machine and said, "Roger, we are warming up the laser now. That pulsing noise you hear is the laser getting prepared."

Roger didn't hear a pulsing noise; he heard a machine-like drum sound beating close by his head and getting louder by the beat. The doctor spoke over this annoying pulsing machine and explained that the nurse was now going to tape the left eye shut while they operated on the right eye. The nurse quickly taped his left eye shut, pulled his right eyelid back and taped it to his forehead and did the same for the lower lid. She then put a speculum over his eye that pulled the flesh back even further and locked itself down around his eye.

The doctor now explained in his best bedside manner, "Roger you will see a red dot in the middle of the light blue circle. It will be pulsing. Just keep your eye focused on this and let us do the rest. We first have to cut the outer layer over the eye and pull the flap back."

"O.K. doc. I promise to focus."

"Next the dot will turn black and the circle white. After that everything turns black and you will feel some pressure in your eye. Don't worry about that, it won't be long. We'll do our thing with the laser and pull the flap back over the eye and then we'll do the left eye. Nothing to it; don't worry."

At this point Roger had a flashback to Judge Brenda Lopez Tyler's Lasik surgery four years ago. She had been in this very surgical center, having the identical surgery, with the identical doctor, with this identical machine. He knew that because he had been dating her at the time and had driven her to the surgical center. He was in the waiting room while she had the laser procedure. The surgical center was very new and had a large glass wall dividing the waiting room and the surgery room. This was a marketing tool that allowed waiting friends and nervous prospective patients watch the procedure performed on others. At the patient's request a curtain could be drawn if they wanted privacy.

Judge Tyler told Roger that she wanted him to watch and that maybe he would have the procedure done one day when he got over being scared. Roger had insisted that it was a private matter and that maybe he shouldn't watch her with her eyes pulled back showing the holes in her skull. Judge Tyler had reminded Roger that he had seen every other orifice in her body and he hadn't seemed to mind.

Reluctantly, Roger agreed to watch. The surgery had started and seemed to be proceeding fine. Unfortunately, neither the doctor nor Judge Tyler knew about the attending nurse's family. Four months before the surgery, Judge Tyler had sentenced the nurse's brother to death for first degree murder.

After the nurse had taped her left eye shut and pulled back the outer flap on Judge Tyler's right eye, the doctor engaged the laser and began the reshaping of her inner eye. The nurse waited until the laser was at the most crucial stage to launch her attack. In one swift motion she turned the intensity level of the laser to high and switched the laser from computer guided to manual. The shocked technicians yelled and the doctor looked up just in time to see the nurse lunge at him and the controls. The doctor fell off his stool and the nurse moved the laser back and forth across Judge Tyler's right eye. Within seconds, the doctor and technicians had pulled the nurse away and turned off the laser.

It was too late. Roger remembered watching through the glass wall while hearing the terrifying screams of Judge Tyler. She jumped off of the table and stumbled blindly around the room with blood coming out of her right eye and down her cheek while her left eye was still taped shut. She looked like a Cyclops that had been struck by a sword thrust and was swinging her arms wildly hoping to stop her unseen attacker.

Ever since the unorthodox assault, Judge Tyler has worn a lavender patch over her useless, right eye and a contact in her left eye. Roger and Judge Tyler stopped dating a few months after the attack, and Roger began dating his current wife, Betty.

Roger came out of his flashback and began looking intently at the red dot. He felt slightly relaxed knowing he had done a

52

complete background check with police computers on everyone in the operating room and cross-referenced it with their family members' criminal background.

Roger felt pressure in his right eye as the red dot changed to a black dot with a white background. He then saw everything go black and the steady drum-like hum of the laser seemed to increase. After a few seconds the black background seemed to have small, brightly colored dots randomly floating. Red, yellow, blue and green dots floated randomly across his black vision like some sort of screen saver on a computer. A burning smell entered Roger's nostril and he nervously asked, "Doc, what's that smell? Is my eye burning? You didn't tell me I would smell my eye. What's wrong, doc?"

"Nothing's wrong. Relax. Some people can smell the laser working. It's all right."

"You didn't tell me I would smell my eye burning, doc. Why didn't you tell me that?" Roger asked as his hands gripped the table tightly.

"Relax. There's nothing wrong. We didn't tell you about the smell because only about 10% of our patients smell the laser. You just have a sensitive nose. It's O.K."

Roger saw a bright gray light, followed closely by a white light with the red dot pulsing in the middle.

"We're done with the right one. Everything is fine."

Roger relaxed and said a silent prayer as they did the procedure on the left eye. After the left eye was done, the annoying drumbeat of the laser stopped as the nurse took off all of the tape and helped Roger to the post-op room.

Roger looked through his freshly reshaped eyes and could tell his vision was better but hazy. The doctor came into the room and explained about all the medicated drops.

"For the first day it will feel like you've been to the beach and gotten sand in your eyes. Don't worry; just keep putting the drops in and sleep as much as possible. Tomorrow your vision should be substantially better. Keep the drops in your eye according to schedule and your vision will be clearer each day. After a week, they should be as good as new."

Roger was pleasantly surprised a week later when his right eye was better than perfect at 20/15 and his left eye was perfect at 20/20. After all of his misgivings and nightmares, Roger had experienced a modern miracle. Judge Tyler had experienced the ancient agony of vengeance.

Chapter 11

Doug woke up from a restful sleep to the phone ringing. As he reached for the phone he noticed the digital clock on his night stand showed 5:25 a.m. He answered groggily, "Hello."

"Detective Shearer, this is Sgt. Busbee. We found two more dead manatees floating by the first span of the Sanibel Causeway. We pulled the beheaded carcasses into the Punta Rassa boat ramp. What should we do next?"

Doug's adrenaline had already pumped through his body. He was wide-awake and shaking with anger as he said, "Secure the carcasses and bring in the divers to look for evidence. I'll be on scene ASAP."

An hour later Doug was parking his Ford truck at the boat ramp as the first rays of dawn peeked over thunderclouds. A brisk north wind made Doug button up his jacket as he walked down towards the sheriff's cars parked by the water.

"Good morning, Sgt. Busbee. What have you found out?"

"Not too much. The divers just got here and they're starting their grid pattern for the dives. It appears the manatees were drugged by some kind of dart from a high-powered rifle. It's the kind vets use to bring down horses or livestock."

Doug looked over at the two dead manatees pulled up on asphalt by the ramp. Their tail flumes were pushed to one side because when they were dragged up the ramp, they folded underneath the rope. Both manatees were adults and measured around 10 feet without their heads. Both of them had a five-inch yellow dart sticking out of their backs. There were a few small shark bites on the shoulder of the manatees, near the cut line on the manatee's neck. Other than the shark bites, the manatees appeared to have the same type of cut as the first three. Their dark gray skin had turned a darker shade around the exposed cut area.

Doug said, "I've seen enough, Sgt., I'm going back to Matlacha to interview Buck Williams. Make sure Dr. Jones gets the carcasses shipped down to his Naples office. Call me later with a report from the dive boat."

As Doug walked back to his truck, he saw a CNN news van pulling into the parking lot. He couldn't believe that Buck Williams was bold enough to keep up his killing spree and taking the heads. As he drove back to Matlacha, he tried to think of a logical reason to take a manatee head. Buck was a die-hard commercial fisherman; if he could make a dollar on something, he would catch it and sell it. Doug couldn't think of any possible use for taking a manatee head other than to piss off the entire civilized world.

As Doug drove to Buck's trailer in Matlacha, he considered the reason two manatees were killed this time and not three. Was someone trying to send a message? Was it a countdown or just a coincidence? Why were darts used this time and not the first time? And most importantly, where were the damn heads?

As Doug drove up to a small group of trailers parked at the end of a dirt road, Buck's son, Carl, stepped out of Buck's trailer. Carl was a tall, lanky man with his mother's red hair and blue eyes. He had a severe farmer's tan on the exposed area outside of his t-shirt. His freckles had blended together with his sunburn, which produced a dark, pink color with patches of dead skin peeling off.

Doug thought back to high school and his first conflict with Carl. When Doug turned 16 he started driving his dad's old truck to school. One day before football practice in their junior year, Carl approached him in the locker room and said, "Doug, I need your help. You know that good-looking blond in science class. She wants me to drive her home because her parents are out of town for the day. Please, can I borrow your truck. I promise I'll bring it back filled up with gas."

Doug replied, "I can't. My dad says I can't lend it out. He'll ground me if he finds out."

Carl stroked Doug's teenage insecurities, "What's the matter, baby face. Do you do everything your parents tell you?"

Doug agreed to let Carl borrow the truck for two hours as long as he had it back before practice was over. Four hours later, Doug is sitting in the dark parking lot at school when Carl rolls up in his truck, followed by another truck. It was making a strained sound that Doug recognized as a transmission problem. Carl said, "I think I might have hit the oilpan on the dirt road. I'm sorry, but you should have told me your oil pan sat low in your truck."

Carl laughed as he got into another truck's passenger door and drove off. Doug had to spend $600 to repair the truck and Carl refused to pay any of the repair bills. After that day, Carl avoided Doug and their friendship disintegrated.

Doug got out of his truck and slowly approached Carl as he said, "How are you doin', Carl?"

Carl's eyes narrowed and he said, "I's doin' a might bit better 'for you showed up. We've been watching T.V. about those dead manatees. You're here to bother my daddy about that, aren't you? Well, he ain't got nothin' to say to you. Unless you got a warrant, you can leave our property."

Doug looked over Carl's shoulder and saw Buck's daughter, Baylee, looking through a part in the old faded curtains. Baylee had her mother's red hair and dark brown freckles, which contrasted with her fair skin. The worry lines on her face diminished the sparkle in her blues eyes. Doug quickly analyzed the situation and changed his tactics.

"Carl, you're right I'm here because of the manatees. But, I'm also here as a friend. The national news media has picked up this story and there is goin' to be tremendous pressure on us to solve this crime. If your daddy can help us with this, we could recommend to the judge a lenient sentence. What do you think?"

Carl looked like he had just sucked a lemon and replied, "We ain't no rats. And besides, we don't know nothin' about nothin'. We ain't killed no damn manatees. But I'll tell you one thing, I ain't gonna shed no tears for those fat bambis. They ain't done nothin' but hurt the fisherman because of these goddamn slow zones. I hope the whole lot of 'em catches some exotic sickness, blow up like beach balls, die and wash up on the tourist beaches. They'd stink worse than some ole' boar hog that got in a fight with a skunk."

Doug was quiet and looked over Carl's shoulder at Baylee and she looked away. Finally, Doug asked, "Carl, what do you use a manatee head for?"

Carl laughed and said, "Fertilizer. For some big fuckin' roses."

Doug realized that there was no chance for cooperation but decided to take a gamble, "Carl, where were you last night?"

Carl snarled, "I's at home reading the damn bible and drinkin' some fuckin' milk. Where were you?"

As Doug turned to walk back to his truck, he said, "Doin' the same thing."

*   *   *   *

Roger turned on the TV as he sat at his kitchen table and ate his pancakes and bacon. He was watching the CBS morning news and the talking head announced, "We have a breaking story in Ft. Myers, Florida. Police have recovered two beheaded manatees floating near the Sanibel Causeway. This comes in wake of three beheaded manatees found one month ago in the same area. The police don't have any comments about the motive."

Roger quickly switched the channel to CNN and saw the reporter at the Punta Rassa boat ramp telling the world about the barbarism in Southwest Florida. He gave a complete history about the gentle mammal as his cameraman zoomed in to show the two headless manatees lying in the sand. It was a revolting image that had the news manager at CNN jumping with joy. Roger left his half-eaten breakfast and quietly dressed for a long day of work.

Chapter 12

Doug spent the morning at his office reassigning his other pending investigations to different detectives at his lieutenant's request. His only assignment was to work on the case against Buck Williams and assist the State Attorney's Office on anything related to it. The media was fascinated by the story and put forth their opinion of the motives for the manatee killings. The speculation from the talking heads on the cable shows ranged from revenge of the recreational boaters to black magic associated with a Santeria cult based in Miami.

After a fast hot dog from *Habits-R-Us*, Doug slowly drove his old Ford pickup down gridlocked U.S. 41 towards the State Attorney's Office in downtown Ft. Myers. The constant stop and go with all of the red lights was starting to wear down the brakes. He reminded himself to call his mechanic, Tommy Hauser, to schedule time for the work. Tommy and his magic tools had kept his 1978 Ford running smoothly all these years.

Doug and Roger had a meeting scheduled with Skip Folly, regional director of biology for the United States Fish and Wildlife Service, at 1:00 p.m. to discuss their response to the attack on the manatees. As Doug waited at a red light, his thoughts drifted to his girlfriend, Mary. He had not seen her since the manatee case had started. She was an easy-going, cute brunette who recently divorced a control freak husband. She wanted time for herself and her friends, which was fine with Doug and his fishing buddies. For the past year, they saw each other once or twice a week depending on their schedules. Lately, Mary had been talking about wanting to have children before she was too old. Doug enjoyed children, but frankly didn't want the responsibility of raising any at this point in his life. Maybe someday, he told himself.

Doug was feeling slightly guilty after spending the past two nights at Amanda's penthouse. Amanda had told him her story of the failed marriage and the yearlong divorce. She did not go into specifics, but apparently her former husband, a real estate developer, had put a lot of property in their joint names which allowed Amanda to exit the marriage with a nice severance package.

As Doug pulled into the parking lot at the State Attorney's Office, his brain shifted gears from the right side and his female problems, to the left side and the logic of law enforcement. On the walk up to Roger's office on the third floor of the courthouse, he saw a few clerks and office workers he hadn't seen since his last case went to trial. After a short time in the noisy waiting room, Roger's secretary brought Doug back to the conference room overlooking the Caloosahatchee River.

Roger got up out of his seat and met him with a handshake, "Good afternoon, Doug," pointed to his left and continued, "This is Skip Folly; he's with the U.S. Fish and Wildlife Service."

Doug turned and watched a small, slightly built man with thin reddish-brown hair rise out of his chair, extend his clammy hand and say, "Nice to meet you, detective. I understand you know the defendant in this matter."

Doug was slightly taken aback by the accusatory tone in Mr. Folly's voice and his damp handshake, but replied in a polite tone, "Nice to meet you, sir. And yes, I went to high school with Mr. William's son."

Mr. Folly's eyes were black, smaller than normal and a little bit too close together. His fair skin was a stark contrast with his black suit, blue shirt and red power tie. Doug became annoyed as Mr. Folly continued to stare at him.

Roger could sense the uneasiness, motioned for everyone to sit down and said, "Well, Doug, the federal government has become extremely concerned with these recent attacks on the manatees. They have decided to immediately put into place emergency, temporary speed zones in all of Lee County. All waters in the county will be a slow zone until a study has been done about how to best protect the manatee."

Doug slammed his hands on the conference table and stood up in shock, "What the hell are you talking about. Just 'cause some old man loses his mind and kills five manatees, we can't use our boats. That's a bunch of bullshit!"

Mr. Folly stood up and pointed at Doug, "That's precisely the attitude we are concerned about. You locals here don't respect the manatee enough. We will make you respect the manatee; the only way to get the attention of all you local yahoos is to implement these emergency procedures."

Roger quickly intervened, "Mr. Folly, let's sit down and talk about this like adults. Doug, please have a seat."

Roger looked at Doug and nodded towards the chair. Roger continued, "These emergency measures are only in effect for 90 days. During that time, additional manatee zones and refuges will be studied. Mr. Folly is going to hold a press conference downtown at the boat ramp at 2:00 p.m. to present these measures to the press. They go in effect tomorrow and the National Guard is being called out to help enforce these laws on the water. They will use their helicopters and coordinate with Coast Guard boats to patrol the water for the next 90 days along with the normal local enforcement."

Doug's face turned red as he shouted, "It'll look like a war zone out there with army helicopters and coast guard boats running around. I can't believe this."

"It is a war zone," Mr. Folly yelled. "Some of your local boaters have attacked our manatees. We will defend this aggression with all of our resources."

Doug and Mr. Folly stared at each other in silence. After a few seconds, Roger said, "All right boys, let's everyone calm down; we're on the same team. Mr. Folly our office is available to help you at any time. Mr. Shearer and I are going to spend the afternoon working on the manatee case. I wish you luck at your press conference."

Mr. Folly looked towards Roger and quickly understood he was being given an easy exit route before Doug slammed him against the wall. After a forced smile, Mr. Folly nodded and left the conference room.

"What is this bullshit, Roger?"

"Settle down, Doug. I'm not happy with it either. It's nothing but a power play. The feds want to put pressure on local law enforcement to do a better job. They want to put pressure on my office to make sure Buck Williams is convicted of every possible charge. And they want to put pressure on the judge to give the maximum sentence."

Doug didn't say anything for a few seconds as he let his blood pressure calm down. He took a deep breath and asked, "Which judge did this get assigned to?"

Roger rolled his eyes and said, "My buddy—the honorable Brenda Lopez Tyler!"

Doug smiled and then started to belly laugh while Roger's face turned red. After a good minute of laughter, Doug asked "Which hotel are you going to have the pre-trial conference in?"

Doug laughed at his own joke and even Roger laughed reluctantly. Finally, it was Roger's turn and he said with a straight face, "Barb Brandon is Buck's defense lawyer."

Doug's smile quickly fell off his face and he felt a headache forming behind his temples while Roger enjoyed a laugh.

Barb Brandon had left the state attorney's office in a highly public dispute with her boss about three years before. During cross-examination on a murder trial, the defense lawyer, Frank Boyle, asked Doug, the lead investigator on the case, what his relationship was with the prosecutor, Barb Brandon. Barb objected loudly and asked Judge Tyler if she could approach the sidebar.

At the sidebar, Barb whispered loudly outside of the jury's hearing, "Judge, this question is irrelevant and highly prejudicial. He is trying to throw mud over the evidence to keep the jury from seeing the truth!"

Judge Tyler rolled her left eye and said, "Ms. Brandon, keep your voice down and save the theatrics for the jury. Now, Mr. Boyle could you explain to me what their relationship is, and how is that possibly related to the case?" Judge Tyler glanced to her left and looked inquisitively at Doug on the witness stand.

Frank Boyle hesitated before answering Judge Tyler. He wasn't sure how relevant the fact was that Barb and Doug had been dating. However, last year he had been at a charity bachelor's auction for the local children's home. Single women made bids for a date with eligible bachelors who volunteered to help the charity. The money went to help the children's home and the women with money to burn got a date with one of the lucky bachelors. Judge Tyler and Barb had bid against each other for a date with Doug. Judge Tyler had won the bidding and went out on a date with Doug. At the end of the date, a drunk Judge Tyler had asked Doug to stay over for the night, but he politely refused. Judge Tyler had called Doug a few times for a second date, but Doug never returned the calls.

Shortly after that, Barb and Doug began dating for real. They had tried to keep their relationship private but the courthouse gossip had linked them together and Frank decided to use this to his advantage. Frank was a seventh generation cracker who was raised on a farm in LaBelle. He came by his southern accent honestly, but it became more distinct, with a bass tone, when performing in court.

After a pregnant pause at the sidebar, Frank slowly whispered, "Judge, it's my undastandin' that the lead investigator who developed this case, Mr. Shearer, and the prosecutrix, Miss Brandon, have been having a sexual thing between 'em. I guess the polite word for it is datin.' Now normally, this'd be a private matter. Howeva, one of the issues in this case is how my client's picture got in the photographic lineup. It's unclear if the police followed proper procedures. If Mr. Shearer, who'd had past dealings with my client, and Miss Brandon were having some pillow talk about possible suspects one night...well...I think the jury should know that."

Barb quickly and loudly said, "Judge that has no relevance to this case."

Judge Tyler's face turned crimson red as she changed her left-eyed gaze to look upon her rival for Doug's affections and then a quick glance at Doug. The lavender patch over her right eye seemed to move forward slightly as if letting off steam. Judge Tyler's figure had expanded since the birth of her two sons and nasty divorce. She still had womanly curves, but they were starting to straighten. She looked at Barb's red Armani suit and couldn't help but think of her toned body filling up the sharp lines. Judge Tyler and Barb's eyes locked as the silence became deafening at the bench.

Finally, Judge Tyler looked up and said to the jury, "Ladies and Gentlemen of the jury, we have some business we need to take care of out of your presence. If you would, please retire for a 10 minute break to the jury room."

After the jury retired, Judge Tyler looked out into the audience area at the victim's family, the defendant's family, support staff from the State Attorney's office and the reporter for the local paper, Peter Hoyem. Judge Tyler said forcefully, "Mr. Boyle has brought to my attention that the witness in this case, Mr. Shearer, and the prosecutor, Ms. Brandon, have been involved in an illicit affair during the investigation of this case. He wants to bring that out to the jury to show some type of bias. My ruling is that the relationship, however unethical it might be, is not relevant to this case and that he may not inquire about it.

"However, I am ordering the court reporter to immediately transcribe this recent exchange at the bench and my ruling on this matter. Once the transcript is prepared, I'm sending it to the Florida Bar. I think Ms. Brandon's conduct should be investigated by the proper authorities." Judge Tyler looked blankly at Barb and said, "Your objection has been granted. We'll start back in five minutes." Judge Tyler left the bench as Peter Hoyem furiously wrote on his note pad.

The next morning the headline in the newspaper, in large bold letters, was *PROSECUTOR AND COP SOLVE MURDER AFTER SEX*. The following day the jury convicted the

defendant, but Barb was asked to resign and she did. The Florida
Bar dismissed the complaint, but Judge Tyler had her revenge.

Chapter 13

It had been one week since the second set of beheaded manatees were found and Doug worked every day since trying to get all the answers to the bizarre crime. After hearing from Skip Folly that all of Lee County was now a temporary slow speed zone for boats, Doug was ready for a fishing break. Doug and Roger had agreed to meet at Doug's house at 3:00 p.m. for some snook fishing in the *Two Tongues*.

Doug woke up from a catnap at 2:45 p.m. and walked over to his refrigerator for a snack. He opened it up and was instantly glad he had asked Roger to pick up subs for dinner on the boat. His survey showed two beers, a coke, tabasco sauce, old swiss cheese with some light purple mold on it and an old pizza box. He opened up the box and saw two pieces of pepperoni pizza shriveled up with the sides of the crust turning yellow. The bad smell hit his nose and he quickly closed the lid. He sat the box down on the counter and checked his cabinet for something edible. He found a can of Vienna sausages, checked the expiration date on the can and opened it up for a snack.

He was finishing the last sausage as he heard the worn brakes on Roger's Buick Regal grinding to a halt. He opened up the garage door and said, "Howdy, Rog. Ya ready to catch some snook tonight?"

"Oh, yeah. I'm ready to drink some beer, too," Roger said as he lifted up the 12-pack from the back seat.

Roger grabbed the beer, chips and subs and walked around the house to the boat. Doug went back inside, locked the garage door and went out the back door to the *Two Tongues*. Doug had already loaded up four snook rods and his tackle box. Roger loaded up the food and drinks in the cooler as Doug untied the lines from the pilings.

As they were idling down the canal Roger said, "I don't want to get your blood pressure up, but remember the speed zone. We've got to go slow the whole way."

Doug grimaced while turning his neck back and forth to try to relieve the immediate stress he felt forming as he said, "There are no manatees in the Matlacha River or Matlacha Pass during March. They're all at the power plant or up canals. You're the lawyer; how can they get away with this bullshit?"

Roger took a deep breath while walking forward to get two beers from the cooler. After he gave one to Doug, he said, "The Endangered Species Act and the Marine Mammal Protection Act are the way they get jurisdiction in state waters. It's their position that there are some poachers hunting the manatees for some weird reason. They think it'll be easier to catch 'em with the slow zones. They also claim that the five manatee killings justify "emergency measures" that don't require hearings or political approval."

Doug said, "Well, we're now in the channel. It normally takes me about 15 minutes to run to the flats off Picnic Island to get bait and then another 5 minutes to run to the docks I like in Tarpon Bay. Let's time it and see how long it'll take."

Roger finished up his first beer and said, "Turn on the radio; we might as well relax on the ride down."

Doug obliged and turned the radio on to his favorite country music station. He tried to relax in his captain's chair, but he could feel his stomach churning with the bitter acid produced by his forced compliance with the slow speed. He concentrated on taking deep breaths and thinking about all of the snook he was going to catch to bring his blood pressure down. The two men sat in silence while riding through the tannin-stained water and watching the sun fall slowly towards the horizon as they enjoyed their beer.

Doug started thinking about the previous night he had spent with his girlfriend, Mary. It was the first time he had seen her since the manatee killings and Amanda coming back into his life. Mary White was a tall brunette with soft, tanned skin stretched

John D. Mills

over her thin body. She ate far too many salads and healthy foods for someone with a good sense of humor. When she laughed, Doug could see the veins in her neck expand out, creating a noticeable curve on either side of her throat outlining her esophagus.

Mary was a schoolteacher that taught fourth grade. She enjoyed teaching her children and was taking night classes at Florida Gulf Coast University to get her Masters in Education. She had been casually dating Doug for the past year and they played house on the weekends if they were available and pretty much did their own thing during the week. The previous weekend Doug had lied and said he had to work overtime when he spent time with Amanda. Mary was missing Doug so she had invited him over on a weeknight for dinner and TV. It was understood that after watching *Jeopardy*, they would retire to Mary's oversized bathtub for the start of their nocturnal recreation.

Doug had arrived at 7:00 p.m. and they ate a healthy dinner of organic salad followed by pasta splashed with low-salt tomato sauce. After dinner, Mary opened up a bottle of White Zinfandel and poured each of them a glass. She turned on *Jeopardy* and walked back to her refrigerator, getting out a small bottle of black olives. Mary loved her olives; she ate them like candy. At first it had amused Doug, but he got where he hated the smell and taste of consumed olives when her kissed her. But it made her happy, and Doug was sure he had some annoying habit that bothered Mary, so he ignored it.

Whenever *Jeopardy* came on, Mary unplugged her phone so she could enjoy her show uninterrupted. Many times Doug would sit next to her and observe her totally contented while eating olives, drinking wine and watching *Jeopardy*. It was not his favorite part of the evening, but it put Mary in a good move so he acted like he enjoyed it.

After *Jeopardy* was over, they moved to the oversized bathtub and Mary's favorite foreplay. As she filled the tub with warm water, she would light dozens of different candles around

68

the tub and put a Barry White CD on the stereo. She turned off all of the other lights in the house and allowed the candle light to give a primitive glow to the bathroom. Mary never allowed more than a few short kisses during their bath together. She enjoyed making Doug wait for anything more passionate until after her bathing ritual.

She first bathed Doug and then he would return the favor while the candles cast flickering shadows as Barry White's music provided a sultry beat. Mary next made Doug lean back against his side of the tub and watch while she conducted her own unorthodox stimulation. She sat up straight in the tub and picked up the nearest candle, pulled it close to her chest and slowly tilted it to the side, allowing the hot melted wax to drip over her small breasts. Her quiet moans of pleasure continued until there was no more melted wax. She set the candle down and lowered herself into the water, wiping the dried wax off her breasts. After this ritual, her sexual frenzy would make Doug forget about the damn olives and just about everything else.

Doug was thinking about the previous night with Mary when he heard Roger laughing next to him in the *Two Tongues.* Roger asked, "What the hell are you thinking about? Your smile is so big your face is wrinkled!"

Doug blushed and replied quietly, "I was thinking about last night with Mary."

Roger asked, "She didn't try to burn you with any of those damn candles, did she?"

Doug laughed and said, "Hell, no. I won't let her get near me with any of those candles. But I like whatever it is they do to her. It was the first time I've seen her since these manatee killings and...well...Amanda is back in town."

"What? You're holding back on me. Give me the dirt, now!"

Doug sighed and said, "O.K. I need your opinion on the whole situation. And besides, we've only gone halfway at slow speed; it's taken us 50 minutes already. We've got plenty of time to play *Dear Abby*.

"Well, she got divorced and moved back to Cape Coral, living in some penthouse on the 18th floor of a condo by the river. She tells me that while the divorce was going on she started dating some guy named Trevor from her country club. She said he wanted to marry her if she would sign a prenuptial. She tells me she would never marry with a prenuptial. She claimed she would always think of how happy we used to be.

"Her story is that she moved back here because she wanted to be near me. That's nice and all, but it doesn't add up. She left me four years ago because she said she didn't want to be married to a cop and live in Ft. Myers. What do you think?"

Roger scratched his chin and said, "You left out the part about how you used to worship her. Women like that."

Doug rolled his eyes, but he knew it was true. He finally spoke up and said, "We've been spending time together at her condo. I've got to admit, I'd forgotten that feeling she gives me. It's addictive."

Roger said, "I remember when you two first moved in together. Amanda wanted a white picket fence around the yard. You built it. Amanda wanted a rose garden so you built one behind the house with eight different types of roses. Amanda wanted new grass, so you put in new sod. You made all of us other married guys look bad in comparison."

Doug said warily, "I remember, I was whipped. But the strange thing was that I liked being whipped."

Roger finished his beer and walked forward for another as he said, "Have fun, just don't let her screw up your mind."

Doug nodded and stood up as the *Two Tongues* approached the intersection with the miserable mile portion of the intercoastal channel. Doug looked to his left, then right and saw a procession of slow moving boats going in opposite directions. The boats appeared to be obeying the new slow zone laws, but Doug could sense the rebellion just under everyone's skin. He crossed over the boat wakes and continued south of Picnic Island to his favorite grass flat for bait. They anchored and started making chum to attract the shiners within castnet range.

Doug first opened two cans of Kozy Kitten cat food and poured it into a bucket. He then opened a can of jack mackerel, pouring it into the bucket while Roger mixed it with his bare hands. He opened a white plastic bottle and added a couple of swigs of menhaden oil to the mess in the bucket. His last secret ingredient was uncooked oatmeal poured into the mix. Roger churned it together until it had the consistency of vomit, not to mention the smell. The smell, along with the fishy mixture floated with the tide, across the grass flats until it crossed path with a school of swimming shiners. The shiners would swim uptide to find the source of the tasty mixture.

While Roger chummed, Doug got out his 10-foot cast net and straightened it out. As Doug put a velcro strip around his wrist and through the loop on the castnet rope he remembered his Dad's death. While Doug was a freshman at Florida State, his father drowned in a freak accident with his castnet. Doug's father was with a friend in his boat throwing his castnet for bait at the Sanibel Causeway. Doug's father threw a 12-foot castnet over a school of bait at the third span of the causeway. The water was 20 feet deep and as the net sunk, it landed on an eight-foot manta ray. The manta ray panicked and quickly swam away. Doug's father was jerked off the boat and pulled behind the fleeing manta ray. The loop knot on the castnet rope closed tight, trapping Doug's father and drowning him. The next day his body surfaced near St. James City with the rope still cinched down around his wrist. The manta ray was exhausted and resting in about six foot of water, still tangled up in the net. The sheriff's office divers cut the rope from the corpse and released the manta ray.

Doug's mother was devastated. She ate very little food and started sleeping more and more. She told Doug that sleep allowed her to dream about Doug's father. She kept taking sleeping pills and not eating well. After two months, she was down to 90 pounds and sleeping 15 hours a day. One day, she finally took all of the sleeping pills in the bottle and entered her last sleep.

Doug tried to remember all of the good times fishing with his father whenever he threw his castnet. It was a learned exercise to keep away the tears.

As soon as he saw the shiners flashing in the chumline, he loaded it up on his arms and threw the net on top of the school. Doug pulled the net in and dumped the school into his livewell. There were well over 200 baits; more than enough for a night of snook fishing.

As the sun was setting, they started slowly motoring towards Tarpon Bay. Roger grabbed the bucket, held it over the side and cleaned it out with the passing water. He filled the bucket up with water and splashed the deck, cleaning the seaweed and chum from the boat. As they pulled into the mouth of Tarpon Bay, the first star of the night appeared in the east, slightly above the half moon that was rising.

Doug said, "It took two hours and twenty minutes to get here. It'd normally take me twenty to twenty-five minutes depending on the wind."

Roger shook his head in disgust as Doug looked at the different docks for a sign of feeding snook. There were no signs of snook strikes so he headed to his favorite dock about half way down the bay. The dock had a boatlift at the end with a large overhead light on a pole about 12 feet above the dock. At the end of the dock four lights were installed under the dock, shining into the water. These snook lights attracted bait fish, which in turn brought in snook. The snook waited in the shadows, facing into the tide and ambushed the bait as the tide pulled them in.

As Doug anchored his boat uptide of the dock, he started swearing to himself.

Roger asked, "What's the problem?"

Doug answered in an irritated tone, "He's put up more barriers for fishermen. The dock owner doesn't like people catching fish from under his dock. For the past few years, he's hung ropes between his pilings at water level to try to stop people from throwing their bait under his dock. That was a pain in the ass, but now he's thrown out crab traps all over the place."

Roger looked around the dock and counted six round Styrofoam floats in the water with attached ropes tied to the pilings as he said, "So are the traps tied under the floats?"

Doug motioned towards the traps and said, "The traps are on bottom. It's about eight feet deep around the dock but he'll have about 15 feet of line tied to the float so it'll drift in the water and hinder fisherman. Then the rope from the float to the piling is in the water creating another barrier.

"You know the thing that really gets me fired up? He has these lights on to attract snook to his dock. He wants the fish to come to his dock but he doesn't want anyone but him to fish for them. What a selfish asshole."

Roger surveyed the traps while thinking of his limited casting ability and asked, "Maybe we should fish a different dock?"

Doug smiled at him and said, "When hell freezes over."

Doug and Roger picked up the five-inch shiners and hooked them through the nose with a small hook so they could swim naturally and attract a hungry snook. Doug threw his bait close to the dock, skipping over the crabtrap ropes while Roger took a more conservative approach and casted up towards shore, away from the entanglements. They both sat down, holding their rods with one hand and drinking cold beer with the other while the country music played quietly in the background. Doug looked towards the west at the high clouds still catching light from the sun that had disappeared over the horizon. The first mosquito of the evening buzzed Doug's ears as he relaxed, waiting on the snook to bite.

The boat on the lift was an offshore boat used to catch grouper and snapper. On the sand, just to the east of the thirty-foot dock, there were three canoes pulled out of the water. One was a standard two-person canoe painted light blue with *Save Our Seacows* painted in black letters on the side. The second canoe was a one-seater painted dark green. The third canoe was a two-seater with a flat end at the rear for a motor mount. It was painted pink and had a five-foot floating stabilizer bar sticking out on each side. It sort of looked like a Polynesian type canoe except there was an electric trolling motor mounted on the rear. The drapes over the big windows on the house were closed but they could see the silhouette of two people walking around in the brightly-lit rooms.

Roger asked, "So...how long ago did you and Barb Brandon date?"

Doug thought for a second and then said, "It was about three years ago. Neither of us wanted anything serious. It was kind of neat to hear the perspective of a former prosecutor who was now a defense lawyer. As you can imagine, we argued a lot."

Roger asked, "So, what happened?"

"No big fight or anything. She went away on a vacation with some of her girlfriends and didn't call when she came back. I didn't call her because it was tarpon season and I was fishing a lot of tournaments with Sandy. Then one night I'm out and I see her in a bar. She introduces me to her new boyfriend, Sean."

Roger smirked and said, "How romantic. The modern couple that's too busy to break up."

Doug shrugged his shoulders and drank the rest of his beer. As he walked to the cooler, Roger asked, "So...how are things with Mary?"

Doug grabbed a fresh beer, wiped ice off the can, pulled open the top and took a long swallow. He sat back down and said, "I guess things are O.K. She's a good woman, but there's no chemistry there. Lately, I've been getting tired of some of her stories and sayings. You know when you've been with someone for a while, they start repeating their favorite stories and using certain sayings over and over. Well, with Mary it's the saying 'a minute-rice moment.'

"Her dad died when she was eight, and she had three younger sisters. Well, her mother obviously had her hands full raising four daughters by herself. Apparently, when her mother started to date again, Mary sort of assumed responsibility for the younger sisters. As she got older, her mother started resenting the fact that her younger sisters listened more to Mary than her. Mary said her mother started criticizing everything she did.

"Well, one day when Mary was seventeen she had taken the grocery list and went shopping. When she came home she helped her mother unpack the groceries. Her mother came across the newly purchased minute-rice and yelled, 'I told you to get regular rice, not minute-rice.' Mary tells me that was the straw that broke the camel's back. She told her mother off and they got in a two-hour fight. She says the minute-rice didn't mean much, but it was what the rice represented that pissed her off.

"So now whenever she has a disagreement or confrontation with someone she says, 'It was a minute-rice moment.'" Doug took a deep breath and continued, "I'm really getting tired of minute-rice moments."

Roger pointed up towards the house said, "I don't know what's going on...but take a look."

Doug turned and looked up at the two silhouettes standing behind the drapes. They moved closer together, embraced and began kissing.

Roger snickered and then a mortar shell exploded behind the boat. At least that's what Roger thought until he realized his bait had been swimming at the surface when a large snook struck the hapless bait. As his line became tight, Roger pulled back and set the hook. The next thing he saw was a snook jump three feet in the air and shake his head furiously. The line from Roger's reel screamed as it was taken off in fast spurts.

Doug said, "Hang on, he's trying to take you to the barnacles. Walk backward and try to pull him out."

Roger walked backward in the boat as his snook jumped and shook its gills while only inches from the barnacles on the pilings. As Roger continued fighting his snook, a second mortar shell exploded under Doug's bait. Doug's snook was only inches from the barnacles and quickly broke the line off. Roger's snook jumped a third time and landed next to the nearest crab trap. Roger felt the added resistance as the snook ran around the crab trap rope and continued pulling. The crab trap float moved a few feet before the weight of the sunken trap caused the rope to become tight. When Roger's snook jumped a fourth time, the line broke off.

"Dammit, I almost had him. That fuckin' rope." Roger yelled.

Doug motioned toward the house and said, "Looks like we disturbed their quality time together."

Roger looked up to the house and could see two men looking through the drapes at them. Roger considered yelling about the rope but thought better of it. Doug and Roger set their rods with broken line in the rod holders and picked up the other two rods, already rigged. They baited up, casted their baits out and immediately had a double hookup. Roger's fish was a keeper at 30 inches and he proudly put it in the cooler. Doug's fish took longer to land and had to be released because it was over-sized at 40 inches. As they were getting new baits, they could see the flashing blue lights of the Sanibel police as they pulled into the driveway of the house.

They continued fishing and soon heard a whining voice coming from the rear door, "That's them, officers. They were up on my dock and I think they're trying to steal something from my boat."

Two uniformed officers walked down the dock while shining their flashlights at the *Two Tongues*. The lead officer said in an authoritative tone, "What are you doing out here?"

Doug answered back, "We're trying to find a cure for cancer. What does it look like we're doing?"

The second officer yelled, "Don't get smart with me, boy or I'll run you in for disturbing the peace. Drive your boat over here and show me some I.D."

Doug and Roger were beside themselves with resentment and anger over their fishing being disturbed. Doug pulled anchor and docked his boat next to the Sanibel officers.

Roger pulled his wallet out and showed them his State Attorney's I.D. as he said, "I'm Roger Bartlett, assistant state attorney and that is Doug Shearer, detective with the Lee County Sheriff's Office. We were fishing and never touched his dock. I want you to call that lying scumbag over here so I can hear him lie to you about seeing us on his dock.

The two Sanibel officers were clearly taken aback and angry. The first one called out to the men standing by the back door, "Mr. Steinworth, can you and your cousin come out here please."

Two tanned, thin men in shorts and sandals walked out on the dock to confront the people disturbing their quality time together. As they approached, the first officer asked, "Mr. Steinworth, what exactly did you see?"

"Well, I saw that boat tied up to my dock and one of these men walking around on my dock, next to my boat. I'm not sure which one."

The lead Sanibel officer asked Steinworth's cousin, "What about you, Mr. Brown. What did you see?"

Brown fidgeted around, looked at Steinworth and mumbled, "Well, I couldn't see too good from my vantage point. I just heard some yelling."

Roger couldn't contain himself any longer and forcefully said, "Mr. Steinworth, my name is Roger Bartlett. I'm a local prosecutor and my friend is a detective with the sheriff's office. I should've waited and let you fill out an affidavit that you saw us on your dock. I then could've prosecuted you for perjury and sent your lying ass to jail.

"You're probably not aware of Florida Statute 372.705 that prohibits harassment of hunters or fishermen. If you interfere with a fisherman taking fish in state waters you are guilty of a second degree misdemeanor punishable by 60 days jail. The water under your dock is public water and we can fish there any time we damn well please. So why don't you and your cousin go back inside and finish whatever family tradition you were practicing."

The Sanibel cops were amused as they watched Steinworth turn white with embarrassment. As Roger was yelling at

Steinworth, Doug remembered his face from the news. Steinworth was the founder and president of *Save Our Seacows*. Doug couldn't resist the temptation so he added, "Mr. Steinworth, I've seen you on TV talking for *Save Our Seacows*. I'm the lead detective on the manatee killings and Roger is the prosecutor on the case. I've heard you demand in TV interviews the maximum sentence for Buck Williams. When you go to jail for harassing a fisherman, should we put you in the same cell with Mr. Williams?"

The Sanibel cops busted out laughing as Steinworth's hands started shaking. Steinworth tried to save face and said, "It was dark and...well...maybe I was mistaken. I'm sorry for the inconvenience. Please, be my guest and fish as long as you would like."

Doug and Roger untied the *Two Tongues* and idled away as Steinworth and his cousin tried to explain their mistake to the smug cops. Doug said loudly enough for the entire group to hear, "Let's go two docks down and get away from those lying scumbags."

Chapter 14

Barb had received some notoriety for her successfully defending a manatee harassment case two years before. After the annual Rancher's Invitational Fishing Tournament at South Bay Resort on Captiva, a maid had found some incriminating Polaroids left over in the room occupied by Tommy "Bubba" Conway. Bubba was a spoiled 30 year-old son of a rich watermelon farmer from Immokalee. The incriminating photos were not the normal sexual ones associated with Polaroids. These were much worse.

There were actually three pictures taken in rapid succession. The first showed Bubba standing on a dock wearing a cowboy hat, rattlesnake boots and nothing else while holding a hose that was shooting fresh water down towards a large manatee that was drinking the treat. The second picture showed Bubba on the manatee's back riding it rodeo style. The third picture showed nothing but Bubba'a cowboy hat floating in the water after the manatee had dove to get away from the threat.

The maid gave the photos to her manager who called the sheriff's office. The police arrested Bubba, but he invoked his right to remain silent and didn't give a statement. The police's attempts to get statements from Bubba's friends at the tournament were fruitless. The friends all did the three-monkey dance: they saw nothing, heard nothing and said nothing.

Barb had successfully defended Bubba in the past over two DUI arrests and a marijuana charge. Bubba's dad retained Barb for the criminal charge of harassing a manatee. The newspapers and TV stations had a field day with the arrest and the trial. The day before the trial, the president of *Save Our Seacows*, George Steinworth, was interviewed by Peter Hoyem of the local paper, and he called for the maximum prison penalty upon conviction.

It took a full day to pick a jury because of all the pre-trial publicity and strong feelings of some potential jurors. At the end of the second day, the state rested its case. Barb successfully argued to the judge that the only direct evidence of the crime was a picture of her client with a manatee. The prosecutor didn't prove when the picture was taken or where it was taken. More specifically, it could have been taken in Columbia, Costa Rica or Brazil, which don't have manatee protection laws. Barb pulled Bubba's passport from her briefcase that showed he had been in all three of those countries in the past year.

The judge reluctantly agreed that the state had not proved that the manatee harassment took place in Florida, and he dismissed the case. George Steinworth was so outraged he and *Save Our Seacows* each pledged to donate ten thousand dollars to the judge's opponent in the next election. Bubba got a lot of press and his status as an eligible bachelor got a phenomenal boost because the Polaroids showed his manhood to be abnormally large. The Ranchers Invitational Fishing Tournament moved their annual event to The Southern Sportsman's Resort in Everglades City that employed more discreet local help.

Barb had been born and raised in Miami. Both of her parents were conservative schoolteachers. Barb inherited their brains but developed her own aggressive traits. She enjoyed drinking as a teenager and took up smoking because her parents told her not to. She went to college and law school at the University of Miami on an academic scholarship. She worked hard and partied hard while in school. She enjoyed bragging that every roommate she had in college or law school flunked out.

After she passed the bar, she took a job as a prosecutor in Ft. Myers. She wanted out of the big city and she enjoyed the beaches of the Gulf coast. After eight years as a prosecutor, she started her own firm specializing in criminal defense. Her legal talents allowed her to live a very affluent lifestyle of a successful career woman.

Chapter 15

Doug was up early getting the *Two Tongues* ready for another trip to gather information for the trial. Doug looked down towards the mouth of his canal and saw the sun rising over the mangrove forest on the horizon. He glanced over at his neighbor's yard and watched in admiration as a great blue heron slowly walked towards a small black snake on the seawall eating a freshly caught lizard. After getting within range the heron's head and long neck shot down and speared the snake. The heron lifted his head up and shook the snake as it squirmed for freedom. After about 15 seconds the heron threw the snake up in the air about a foot and caught it head first in its open mouth. The heron's neck expanded to allow the still struggling snake to slide down towards its digestive juices percolating in its hungry stomach. Doug smiled as he pondered how Mother Nature could be cruel and beautiful at the same time.

The morning silence was broken by Roger's noisy Buick Regal as he parked in Doug's drive. The blue heron squawked loudly as he took flight towards the rising sun. Roger came huffing into the backyard balancing a cup of coffee and apologized for being late as he loaded his duffel bag into the *Two Tongues*.

As they idled down the canal Roger said, "You won't believe the new case we got in the office this week. It happened downtown at the boatshow. Apparently, Raytheon has these new nightvision binoculars on the market. Some of the boat salesmen had borrowed one from a Raytheon sales rep and were having a good 'ole time. The nightvision binoculars detect heat and produce an image based on the heat level. Well, one of the salesmen got the idea of trying it out during the day. You won't believe what the damn things can see.

"Normally a human shows up as red or bright orange when viewed. But fake boobs show up as blue! So all of these guys

81

are looking at the women and can see who has fake tits. Of course, this tidbit of information spreads like wildfire and there are lines of hungry men waiting to look through the binoculars.

"As you can imagine, eventually the women at the show hear about the binoculars and they go ballistic. One blond bombshell in an orange bikini top and white hot pants tells her muscle bound boyfriend about the old guys looking at her huge fake boobs. He starts a fight and all hell breaks loose. The cops are called and arrest four guys for battery. I think I'll offer to drop the charges if they forfeit the binoculars to me."

Doug laughed and asked, "What else is happening downtown?"

Roger thought as he took a drink of his warm coffee and watched a flock of pelicans flying in formation above the houses. He chuckled to himself and then said, "Everybody in the office is upset with the new proposed drugs tests. There are two types of tests that everybody is fighting over. Upper management wants to test the hair of all employees. If you have ever done drugs it shows up in your hair. Most people want to have urine tests; they only register if you have done anything in the past 30 days."

Doug asked, "Does it matter to you one way or the other?"

"No, I don't care; I've never done any drugs. However, I have tested positive for biscuits and gravy," Roger said as he patted his belly.

Doug laughed as he looked at his friend sitting contently in the passenger seat. Roger always made fun of his heavy frame, but Doug suspected it was a painful subject for him.

Doug asked, "Any good trial going on?"

Roger answered, "They've got this wild trial going on down in the civil division. This retired engineer moves into one of those expensive, gated communities down in Bonita Springs. Well, apparently he gets bored and decides to do a little snooping around the neighborhood. But he's a smart guy with a little money. He buys this high-tech listening equipment that allows you to hear through walls. It kinda looks like a mini-umbrella that's clear. You aim it at the place you want to listen and you can hear through walls up to 200 feet.

"So this guy gets his jollies by riding his three wheel bicycle around the neighborhood at night listening to his neighbors do the wild thing. He puts all the equipment in the basket behind the seat. But he doesn't just listen; he makes tapes of the good stuff. Well, one night a security guard catches him in the act. The engineer comes clean with the security guard and makes a deal with him. If the security guard doesn't turn him in to the authorities, he'll let him listen to the tapes.

"So, the engineer gives the security guard some of the tapes to take with him. As you can imagine, it was such juicy material the security guard lets one of his other guard buddies listen to it. Well, the second guard gets disgusted by it and calls the cops. The cops confiscate all of the tapes and bring it to us for prosecution, but we decline to prosecute because everything the engineer had was legal. However, all of the neighbors hire a civil lawyer to sue him for invasion of privacy. The case has been going on all week. It's better than a soap opera."

Doug laughed and said, "I guess Big Brother isn't just watching; he's listening."

As they exited Doug's canal and entered the Matlacha River, Roger said, "Well the federal emergency measures have been in effect for a week. All waters in Lee County are now a slow zone."

Doug nodded and said, "Everybody on the island has been calling me and complaining. They think that because I work for the sheriff I'm responsible for making these laws. People are gettin' so mad they're gonna start attacking the manatees. Wouldn't that be ironic; increased manatee zones and increased enforcement cause the manatee population to go down. One guy told me he heard a couple of guys at the fish house talking about putting poison in heads of lettuce and throwing them in the water at the manatee park over by the power plant where all of the manatees are congregated."

Roger shook his head back and forth while rolling his eyes and said, "Non-boaters don't understand how burdensome these laws are to boaters and fisherman. Can you imagine if someone declared love bugs were an endangered species. The equivalent law would be that no one could travel on roads over 25 mph. Some roads close to fields and agricultural land would be declared a no-drive zone during the summer months when the love bugs breed. I wonder how long the voters would put up with that?"

Roger answered his own question, "Not long. I'll tell you something else. All of the Wildlife officers I've talked to are against the increased regulations. The manatees were increasing with the old regulations and now they have the nightmare of forcing boaters to comply with these news laws. They think the speed zones increase the chance of fatal boating accidents for humans because 60-foot yachts are running next to 12-foot johnboats with kids in them.

"I've got another treat for you. One of the Wildlife officers told me he was at a seminar last summer and one of the instructors said that within 10 years they were going to try to restrict days boaters could use their boat. If your boat registration number ends in an odd number you could only boat on Monday, Wednesday, Friday and Sunday. Even numbers would have the other days and they would change schedules every other year. How about that bullshit?"

Doug drove in stunned silence as the *Two Tongues* slowly plowed through the steady chop caused by a 10-mph northwest wind. Roger opened up his duffel bag and pulled out a battery operated flashing blue light as he said, "We use these on undercover cars. I was reading the regulations on these emergency measures yesterday. There is an exception for law enforcement vessels. Therefore, I commandeer the *Two Tongues* for law enforcement today."

Doug smiled as Roger walked forward and secured the suction cups on the bottom of the flashing light to the bow.

Roger came back to his seat, drained the last of his coffee and said, "Take it to warp speed, captain."

Doug smiled and pushed the throttle down steadily as he looked at the other boats going slow in the channel. The Yamaha engine purred as it pushed the *Two Tongues* through the heavy waves. Doug pulled the throttle back slightly and lowered his trim tabs so his bow could absorb the waves better. The speedometer showed they were going 38 mph as they left the Matlacha River and entered Charlotte Harbor. Doug drove in silence and loved the feeling of air racing over his face as he surveyed all of the water rushing by.

After about 10 minutes of boating freedom, Doug heard a loud *Thud-Thud-Thud* noise coming from behind him and increasing in volume every second. As he instinctively turned his head, he saw three green helicopters bearing down on him in attack formation. They buzzed him, made a wide turn and vectored in to face Doug.

"Stop the boat," the loudspeaker from the lead helicopter bellowed.

Doug immediately pulled the throttle back and the boat came off plane, drifting slowly towards the helicopters. He could now see *U.S. ARMY* written in white lettering on the sides. Doug next heard the whining of outboard engines being pushed to their limits. He looked to his left, then right and saw a Coast Guard boat rapidly approaching. It was a 25-foot Boston Whaler rigged with twin Johnson engines and a T-top adorned with all of the latest radar and GPS technology. Four Coast Guard officers were on the boat as it continued speeding towards Doug on a collision course. The *Thud-Thud-Thud* noise was alarming as the helicopters hovered less than 20 feet above the water while holding less than 100 feet away, still in attack formation. Doug looked back at the Coast Guard boat as it came off plane approximately 50 feet from him and drifted rapidly towards his boat.

Doug yelled, "What the hell are you doing?"

The Coast Guard captain picked up his bullhorn and ordered, "Put your hands up where I can see them. We're going to board you."

The Coast Guard boat continued its dangerous approach as two of the officers grabbed rubber buoys to place between the boats. Doug noticed the third officer with his M-16 aimed at his head and immediately put up his hands. The two officers barely threw the buoys over the side before they cushioned the collision between the boats, which bounced apart a couple of feet. The captain threw the engines into reverse, turned the wheel and backed down quickly allowing the two officers to promptly tie the boats together. The third officer kept Doug in his M-16 sights.

The Captain looked Doug and Roger over, inspected the boat for weapons and yelled, "You're impersonating a law enforcement boat; that's a felony."

Doug yelled back, "We are law enforcement, you idiot. Take your gun off me and I'll show you my badge."

The captain motioned for the officer to lower his M-16, looked at Doug and said, "Show me your I.D. Why are you in a civilian boat?"

Doug produced his badge and passed it to the captain as he said, "This is my personal boat. My friend here is the prosecutor on the manatee killings and I'm the detective assigned to it. We're going to the areas where the carcasses were found to time how long it would've taken the suspect to drive between the three points."

The Coast Guard captain got on his radio and sent the Army helicopters away to search for other speeders in the manatee zones. He then motioned toward the blinking blue light on the front of the *Two Tongues* and asked sarcastically, "Where did you get that piece of equipment?"

Roger raised his voice and answered in an annoyed tone, "Off an investigator's car. They're perfectly legal."

The Coast Guard captain chuckled to himself and said in a bothered voice, "Whatever. You guys have fun with your joy ride."

As the Coast Guard boat drove away, Doug and Roger sat down and tried to control their growing anger. Doug finally spoke in a quiet voice, "That is the damnedest thing I've ever seen in my life. A federal posse in Pine Island Sound enforcing manatee slow zones. It's not right what these people are doing. It reminds me of the saying, 'Hi, I'm from the federal government, and I'm here to help you.'"

Roger didn't say anything as Doug pushed the throttle forward, holding it down to get every ounce of horsepower from his engine. The *Two Tongues* sliced through the deeper, rough water and leveled off at 52 mph as he raced over the smaller waves on the flats northwest of Bokeelia. Doug kept the throttle down as they raced across Pine Island Sound towards Buck key. It took 18 minutes at full throttle to reach the spot where the first carcass was found and Doug enjoyed every second of the ride.

After they came off plane Roger finally spoke up, "What I want you to do is time how long it takes to get from Buck key, where they found the first manatee, to McIntire Creek, where the second manatee was found, going slow. After that we'll ride up McIntire Creek to Ding Darling where they found the third manatee, the baby. Then on the way back to Buck key, I want you to go thirty. We calculated that is the maximum speed of Buck William's boat. I want to have the speed and distance documented in case his lawyer tries some bullshit defense that he couldn't have done all three."

Doug asked, "She's pushing this case by filing a demand for speedy trial. What do you think her defense is?"

Roger replied, "I have no idea. The DNA tests have come back. The manatee flesh from the chainsaw matched all three manatees; therefore, he killed all three. We don't know all the details, but it doesn't matter. We have the best circumstantial case I've ever seen. The only thing we're missing is a confession."

Doug and Roger looked up and saw a canoe with two men paddling towards them. Doug got two diet Cokes out of the cooler as they relaxed before documenting the times between the crime scenes. The canoe drifted up next to them and one of the men asked in a demanding tone, "Why were you speeding across the slow zone?"

Doug remembered the voice, recognized the canoe and said, "Mr. Steinworth, as you know, my friend Roger is the prosecutor on the manatee case and I'm the detective assigned. We're gathering evidence for the trial. I assume you and *Save Our Seacows* would approve."

Steinworth said, "Of course; I didn't recognize you." He hesitated and continued, "I'm sorry about my mistake the other night at my dock."

Doug forced himself to reply, "Oh, don't worry about it. Maybe we were a little too loud."

Steinworth and his alleged cousin waived goodbye and started paddling towards Tarpon Bay. As they were leaving, Steinworth turned and shouted, "Isn't it a glorious day. I can canoe in peace without worrying about waves from boats."

Doug watched the tandem paddle off, sighed and said, "Let's get started. I'm meeting Amanda at Big Papa's for a steak dinner. I don't want to be late."

Doug and Roger measured the time and distance between the three crime scenes and drove back towards Matlacha, passing all the other boats going slow. Roger left and headed home while Doug cleaned up the boat. Doug went inside to shower as the sun was falling fast and the seabreeze was increasing. While showering, Doug thought of Amanda and their last, rigorous night together at her penthouse. Doug put on Amanda's favorite cologne and dressed in jeans with a yellow Columbia fishing shirt.

Doug drove into Big Papa's driveway promptly at 6:00 p.m. and saw him loading up the charcoal on his grill made out of a 55-gallon drum sliced in half. As Big Papa poured the lighter fluid on the charcoal, Doug walked over to the ever-present cooler on the picnic table and grabbed a beer. He opened up the cold beer and savored the taste as it went down. Doug could tell this was going to be a night to let Amanda drive him home.

"Amanda called a little while ago; gonna be late. What a surprise, huh?" asked Big Papa as he lit the fire.

Doug smiled and said, "Oh, well."

Big Papa walked over to the picnic table and picked up his plastic cup and took a long drink. He then asked, "You gonna stick with beer or ya want some Lord Calvert?"

Doug smiled meekly and said quietly, "I haven't talked to the Lord since that night we drank some and talked about Sandy's killer."

Big Papa's face darkened and he took a big swallow from his drink. He took a deep breath and said, "A pull from a drink is good for the soul. Let's go inside and let ya have a talk with the Lord. If I 'member right, some good things happened after ya last drank some. Remember, the Lord works in mysterious ways."

Big Papa smiled warmly at Doug and motioned for him to come inside. Doug lifted up his beer, drained it and followed. Big Papa opened up his old freezer and took out an ice tray, emptying it into an oversized plastic cup. He filled it half with Lord Calvert and half with ginger ale, stirring it with a knife that was lying on the kitchen counter. Doug picked up the industrial-sized drink and took a big pull from the potent mixture. He relaxed and asked, "Where's Hannah?"

Big Papa said, "She's in heat. I think she's been sneakin' off down the street to see the neighbor's Great Dane."

Doug replied, "I guess that's better than a toy poodle!"

Big Papa laughed and said, "Where there's a will, there's a way."

Both men sat down at the kitchen table and drank some more. Doug noticed that the newspaper was opened to the obituary page and asked, "Did someone you know die?"

Big Papa's eyes suddenly looked very tired and said quietly, "Son, when you're my age you read the obituary page everyday.

It's kinda like current events for old people—chances are someone you know is going to be there."

Big Papa laughed quietly to himself and said, "Did you hear the one about the engaged couple that died in a car wreck the weekend before their wedding?"

Doug nodded negatively and Big Papa continued, "They're at the pearly gates and they ask St. Peter if it was possible to get married in heaven. St. Peter scratched his head and said, 'I'm not sure but wait at the gate and I'll find out.' Two days later St. Peter showed back up and said, 'I confirmed that it was possible to get married in heaven.' While St. Peter had been gone, the young couple talked about what would happen if they weren't happy with marriage. So, the husband asks St. Peter, 'If the marriage doesn't work out, is it possible to get divorced?' St. Peter gets mad and throws down his note pad and says, 'It took me two days to find a priest. How long do you think it'll take me to find a divorce lawyer?'"

Both men laughed and the jokes started flowing as freely as the drinks. As they were telling dirty jokes a shrill voice cried out, "Too noisy; quiet! Too noisy; quiet!"

Big Papa turned and looked at a bright green parrot on a perch in the den and yelled playfully, "Oh, shut up Hamlet. We're just having fun."

Hamlet fluttered her wings and squawked. Doug said, "I forgot about Hamlet. How old is she now?"

"Well, Terri and I got her about seven years ago. Terri died three years and two months ago and...I've...been..." Big Papa was choking up and he tried to hold back his tears. He took a deep breath and looked over Doug's shoulder, staring at some unknown spot on the wall and continued, "Hamlet is all I've got left to remind me of Terri. Ya know, when you're married to a woman for 38 years and ya raise two good kids...well...when she dies...it's not easy on an old man."

Big Papa took a long drink as he stopped trying to hold back his tears. He walked over to the counter and tore off a piece of paper towel, wiping his eyes. Doug wiped his own tears on the back of his hand and took a long drink as an awkward silence formed. Big Papa took a deep breath and continued, "Ya know, late at night Hamlet and I have talks. Sometimes, Terri comes down and visits with us. I don't know why; maybe God feels sorry for a lonely old man. It's so nice to talk to her. She tells me how beautiful it is in heaven and that she misses me. And..," Big Papa started crying and walked over for another paper towel.

Doug took another long drink and waited. After Big Papa wiped his tears away with a trembling hand and blew his nose, he continued, "We talk about all of our friends that she talks to in heaven. It's kinda embarrassin' but she reminds me to take a bath. Ya know, since I live alone, sometimes I don't shower every day; being just me. Well, she reminds me to shower and eat my vegetables."

Big Papa took a deep breath, followed by a long drink and continued, "She tells me she sees Sandy every day, and he asks about me. But Sandy never is allowed to come talk to me." Big Papa coughed and cleared his throat before he continued, "Why do you think God lets an old man talk to his dead wife, but not his dead son?"

Big Papa stopped talking and started looking at the unknown spot on the wall that allowed him to communicate with his dead wife. Doug looked at Big Papa and watched the tears run down his face and drip on his flannel shirt. Doug wondered if he would ever find a woman that loved him that much.

After a few quiet moments, Big Papa looked over at Doug, took a pull on his drink and said, "Well, let's go check on the fire. If Amanda walked in and saw us crying like this...she'd think we're watching some Oprah reruns."

Doug laughed and followed Big Papa out into the cool night to check on the fire. After spreading out the coals, they sat down at the picnic table and stared at the fire. After a few seconds of relaxing and enjoying the numbing effects of the drink, Big Papa asked, "So how are you and Amanda gettin' along?"

Doug sighed and looked Big Papa squarely in the eyes, "You know I'll always love Amanda. But when she walked out on me back then, well, something changed. I don't know. She married that rich guy 'cause she wanted a life I couldn't provide her. She tells me that during the divorce she started datin' some retired rich guy from her country club, but she kept thinking of me. I don't know what to think."

Big Papa chuckled and said, "I love her to death, but she's always been the selfish type. I remember when she was eight years old she got in trouble at Sunday school. The teacher spent the whole hour talking about Jezebel and all of her problems. Well, at the end of the lesson, little Amanda blurts out, 'I want to be like Jezebel. She's cool.' Well, as you can imagine the kids all laughed and the teacher got pissed. I think we stopped going to Sunday school after that.

"Even at an early age her mother and I could see her looks would spoil her. Sure enough, as she grew up and turned into a beautiful woman, the guys fell all over themselves trying to make her happy. If Amanda had been Helen of Troy, she'd have been insulted that only one thousand ships were launched for her."

Doug laughed and said, "Then we started dating. I think she loved me but that somehow I was too ordinary for her. I don't know what to think."

Big Papa chuckled, "When I was a young man, things were a little simpler. If a man and a woman loved each other, that was enough. Why isn't that enough anymore?"

Doug thought for a second before he answered, "Today's media bombards us with all of the latest in fashion, gossip, and style. The advertisers try to send us the message that if we don't buy their stuff, we aren't successful. Unfortunately, that sometimes influences people's definition of happiness. The great search for success. What is success?"

Doug's question went unanswered as the two men looked up at the bright stars. As Doug and Big Papa took a drink, they heard Amanda's Porsche downshifting as she slowed to turn in his drive. She drove up in her metallic silver, convertible Boxster and slid to a stop, sending gravel flying. Amanda got out of the car and said, "Isn't this a sight. I guess you've solved all of the world's problems today."

Amanda walked over, hugged her Dad, gave Doug a kiss and sat down next to him. Big Papa asked, "So why are you so late, honey?"

Amanda answered, "I went shopping with a girlfriend down to the Waterside Shops in Naples. You wouldn't believe the traffic. I can't believe how many people there are in Naples and Ft. Myers."

Big Papa said, "When I was young, Ft. Myers was so small you didn't loose your girlfriend; you just lost your turn."

"Daddy!"

Doug and Big Papa laughed as Amanda blushed. She opened her purse and took out a cigarette, lighting up. Big Papa said, "You really should stop smokin' honey."

Amanda shrugged her shoulders and said, "At least it's fat free."

Big Papa excused himself and went inside to get the steaks. Amanda touched Doug on the arm and said, "Boy, do I have some juicy gossip. My girlfriend told me that Marianne Black is dating a gynecologist. Can you imagine? A gyno is always with another woman. Everyday!"

Doug wasn't sure what to say as Amanda laughed at her own joke and continued, "My girlfriend was wearing a turtleneck today. I just absolutely hate turtlenecks and hats. I guess I must've been a witch in a former life."

Amanda laughed, looked at Doug's puzzled face and said, "Loosen up, Dougie."

She slid closer to Doug and hugged him. She kissed his neck while sliding her hand down his stomach and whispered, "Eat a big meal, lover. You're going to need your strength tonight."

Chapter 16

Doug's cell phone rang as he was driving down U.S. 41 towards the State Attorney's Office in downtown Ft. Myers.

"Hello."

Mary said, "Howdy, stranger. I haven't heard from you lately. I was wondering how you're doing."

Doug slammed on his brakes to avoid a collision with a Pontiac Bonneville driven by a Q-tip and dropped his phone. He said, "I'm sorry, I dropped the phone. Some old, white-haired lady cut into my lane without even looking. Damn near caused a wreck."

Mary laughed and said, "I think they're worse than teenage hotrods. At least with hotrods you can predict their behavior. They're going to go fast and cut you off. With Q-tips they can barely see over the wheel and they have no idea about anyone else on the road."

Doug said, "Oh well, the price we pay to live in paradise. So what's going on?"

Mary said, "I miss you. You've been working so much, I hardly ever see you except when you're being interviewed on TV. I wanted to see you tonight."

Doug thought quickly and lied, "I'm sorry. I've got a meeting tonight with the other detectives to discuss pending cases. Maybe Sunday night."

Mary was quiet for a few long seconds and finally said, "Sounds like prime time is taken. I guess I get reruns on Sunday."

Doug said, "I'm sorry, I've got so much going on. I miss you, though."

Mary was encouraged and said, "I miss you, too. I guess I'm a little emotional because I visited with my friend today and her two kids. I had so much fun playing with them. It got me thinking, I'm not getting any younger. You know what I mean."

The hair on the back of Doug's neck stood up as he realized Mary's biological clock had kicked into hyperdrive. He measured his words carefully and said, "I'm glad her kids are doing well. Maybe you could take them to the park this weekend."

Mary said in a disappointed voice, "Yeah, maybe I will. I'll talk to ya later, Doug."

Doug heard the click on the line as Mary abruptly ended their conversation by hanging up. It was not pretty, but Doug had accomplished his goal of ignoring Mary's suggestion of commitment and kids. Doug forced himself to forget about Mary and focus on his afternoon meeting with Roger at the State Attorney's Office.

Within ten minutes, Doug was weaving his way through the mass of workers at the State Attorney's office. He finally entered Roger's corner office with a window looking over the Caloosahatchee River and said, "How many people do you have working in the office?"

"We've got over 220 people working for us through the circuit; here in Ft. Myers we have 104," Roger answered as he got up out of his chair and shook Doug's hand. He shut his door and when he sat back down a shirt button, covering his stomach, popped off and landed on his desk. Red-faced, Roger yelled, "That's it! Time for a diet, I'm sick of being this heavy."

Doug was embarrassed for his friend so he was quiet as Roger slowly rubbed his neck with his right hand. Finally Roger said, "Just what I need—starting a diet as I'm preparing for a trial with the highest media coverage of my career. Great. Just fuckin' great."

Doug tried to ease the tension and said, "Well look at the bright side. All of the evidence is in your favor. We caught the defendant with one of the dead manatees. All three manatee's DNA is on the chainsaw that was found in his boat. The only fingerprints on the chainsaw were the defendant's. We've got him cold."

"That's what worries me. Why does he want a speedy trial if he's so guilty? How does he think he can beat this case? I wonder if he'll try to show that since we can't prove he was connected to the second set of killings, he didn't do the first?" Roger asked.

Doug rolled his eyes and said, "I bet it's his lawyer that wants the trial. Win, lose or draw, Barb loves the publicity. Remember a few years ago when she got 'ole Bubba Conway off on that manatee charge. She was doing talk shows and radio shows weeks after the case was over. She's just trying to play this out. She knows he's guilty as hell, but it'll be a good show for the networks."

Roger sighed, leaned back in his chair, showing his hairy belly through the gap caused by his missing button, and said, "I don't know what to think. We're starting trial in two weeks. All of my witnesses are subpoenaed, all of my evidence is ready, all the testing is done and all the exhibits are prepared. I can't imagine what his defense will be."

Doug asked, "Have you decided if you are going to try to use the second set of killings?"

Roger answered, "Not directly, there's no way I can tie them to Buck. It might backfire on me. Barb will try to say that proves there are other killers out there."

Doug shrugged and consoled his friend, "You've done everything there is to do. Twice. You're ready for trial, just relax."

"You're right," Roger said as he slowly nodded his head. He took a deep breath and continued, "I do have an unusual assignment for us tonight. Skip Folly, your buddy from U.S. Fish and Wildlife, is having a workshop tonight at 6:30 p.m. at Harborside Convention Hall for public imput on additional manatee sanctuaries and refuges. We are suppose to accompany him for any assistance he might need."

Doug frowned and closed his eyes as he said, "You've got to be kidding me. I hate this jerk, and now I've got to act like I support him at this meeting while all my friends and neighbors are going to be there raising hell about these new regulations."

Roger was quiet as Doug stood up and paced around the office. Doug finally said, "I don't know if I can do this. I hate this guy."

Roger said, "I understand how you feel. I've got an idea; let's go to the Veranda for drinks at happy hour and take the edge off before we go over to Harborside."

The Veranda was downtown Ft. Myers' oldest and most elegant restaurant and bar. Many lawyers, bankers and businessmen were drawn to the old plantation house for happy hour. Many court cases were settled and business deals finalized in the wood-paneled bar as the falling sun sent reflections through the beveled glass windows. Many romances blossomed as the lights dimmed and the drinks flowed while Lila played the baby grand piano to perfection.

Doug and Roger walked up the brick steps to the Veranda as they were debating the exact family heritage of Skip Folly. When they opened the door they could hear the lively conversation from the happy hour crowd. They walked over to a small table next to the fireplace and sat down in the green high-backed chairs.

After the waitress brought Doug a double shot of Lord Calvert and Roger a glass of Diet Coke, Roger asked, "Have you ever been to one of these public comment workshops before?"

Doug said, "I went to one a few years back when they were doing the state netting laws. It was such a joke. These government bureaucrats sit up front and let each person talk for three minutes to give their imput. They don't listen; they've already decided what they're going to do."

Roger nodded and said, "That's what I figured. But the big wigs want us to show up. Keep up appearances and all. I've a hard time trying to explain these new proposals to my neighbors. It's like when you have a bad case, but the boss wants you to take the case to court and let the jury decide. I've walked a few dogs in front of juries. You never know what a jury will do."

Doug said, "You know, most juries are pretty smart. I was talking to one of my neighbors one time after he served on a jury, and he told me how they decided the case. He said, 'Each side brought their liars and we decided who was lying the least.'"

Roger laughed and finished his Diet Coke. He flagged down the waitress, ordered another round and asked Doug, "Why do you have those bags under your eyes? Did Amanda or Mary keep you up last night?"

Doug smirked and said, "Neither. My weekly report at the sheriff's office had to be logged in on the computer by 2 a.m. I'm a nightowl and a procrastinator—it's a bad combination."

After two drinks, Doug and Roger walked over to Harborside to greet Skip Folly. They walked in to the convention hall and saw many friends that cornered them asking about the new regulations. After 20 minutes of trying to answer the questions, they excused themselves and found Skip in the hospitality room. He was drinking a crème soda and eating chocolate-chip cookies.

Skip saw them, walked over and said, "I hate these things. But the regulations say we have to listen to these idiots. We've already drawn up our plan but we can't unveil it until we let these guys run off at the mouth."

Doug thought about giving Skip a piece of his mind but held back. Roger tried to be a diplomat and said, "This is a very important topic to people. It affects their livlihood and their pleasure. Don't you think you should at least listen to what they have to say."

Skip sniffed, scratched his chin and said, "We know what's best. I don't give a damn about these people and all their whining." He pulled his hands together, cracked his knuckles and continued, "I need to go up front and sit at the head table so we can get started. I appreciate your agency supporting us here tonight."

Roger and Doug looked at each other in disgust as Skip walked up front to the speaker's table. There were over 300 people in the convention hall looking at all of the displays on the back wall showing the different manatee zones. Skip banged his gavel and said into the microphone, "Everyone please be seated, we need to get started. We have over 60 people that have signed up for comments tonight. Because of time constraints each person will be limited to two minutes.

"The first speaker is Steve Saylor, president of *Save Our Speed*. Please approach the microphone and speak quickly. You only have two minutes."

Saylor approached the microphone and said, "My question won't take two minutes, but your answer might. Why do we need additional manatee regulations when the total manatee population has increased by 45% in the past three years?"

There were immediate echos through the audience of "Yeah, answer that," and "You got that right."

Skip waited until the ruckus calmed down and smugly said, "We're only here for comments. We're not hear to answer questions."

Saylor would not be brushed aside by the government bureaucrat so easily and said, "If that's true, why did you invite *Save Our Seacows* to your manatee conference in Tallahassee and not my group *Save Our Speed*?"

Skip looked at Saylor and said, "Apparently, you have problems understanding the English language. I will repeat again that we're not here to answer questions but only to get public comment." Skip and Saylor stared at each other for a few seconds and then Skip firmly said, "The next speaker is Capt. Duke Godfrey from Captiva."

Captain Godfrey slowly approached the microphone and said in a cracking voice, "When my clients won't pay me to take them fishing anymore because it takes so long to drive to the fishin' spots, what do I do?"

Skip appeared bored as he spoke in his mechanical voice, "We're only taking comments, not answering questions. Next."

Carl Williams walked rapidly towards the stand and grabbed the microphone from the holder, "I'll tell ya one thing, ya city-slicker carpet bagger—don't stick your nose where it don't belong. If you people don't leave us alone, we're gonna have one big manatee Bar-B-Q and we won't hav' ta worry about 'em any more."

Carl noisily put the microphone back into the holder as a few radicals clapped for him. The rest of the crowd was silent because they realized that he played into the propaganda promoted by *Save Our Seacows*.

Skip announced, "The next speaker is Kenny Oswald."

Oswald was wearing faded old jeans and a dark blue t-shirt with bleach stains. He slowly approached the microphone and looked around the room before he started, "Everyone here in this room knows what's going on. The government is tryin' to get rid of the commercial fisherman. They ain't got no need for us and they want our waterfront land. And the son-of-a-bitches might get it, cause we can't afford to fight 'em. Mr. Folly, I just want ya to know, we know what you're doing. You've declared war on our way of life. We might loose the war, but we're gonna take some of you bastards with us."

There was a loud rumbling and sporadic swearing in the crowd. For the next two hours people spoke and asked questions to the well-rehearsed government bureaucrat, Skip Folly. By the end of the meeting, a wave of anger, discontent and rebellion swept through the crowd. Most people swore under their breath but left the meeting peacefully.

Three members of *Save Our Speed* waited for Skip to exit the platform and walk past them. Doug and Roger saw them staring at Skip, waiting at the only exit from the hall. They decided to accompany Skip as he approached the angry threesome.

Steve Saylor spoke first, "When are we going to get our questions answered?"

Skip answered, "I will let my superiors in D.C. know your concerns."

Mark Shaw spoke in a loud voice, "You people don't give a damn about what we say. You're going to do whatever you want, aren't you?"

Skip said in a mocking manner, "Of course we're going to listen to your group. You like to drive fast in your expensive boats and run over manatees. Your opinion is very important to us when we try to protect the manatee."

Finally the third member of *Save Our Speed*, Bubba Conway, stepped in front of Skip, pointed his finger at his face and said, "You act like we're criminals. All we want to do is ride in our boats and fish."

Skip stepped back, threw up his hands and spoke forcefully, "All right, enough of this intimidation bullshit. You people say we treat you like criminals. If you mess with the feds, we'll make all of you criminals."

Skip looked at everyone's skeptical face and continued, "You don't think so? Well, let me explain it to you real simple, so you can understand. First of all, with your bad attitudes, it's likely that most of you have been through a divorce. We'll get your financial affidavit from your divorce file and compare it to all of your loan applications. I bet that loan from your uncle you listed on your divorce financial affidavit is conveniently missing from your bank application. Boom! We've got you on bank fraud.

"After we arrest you at your house, on a Saturday morning at 7 a.m. in front of your family and neighbors, we'll get a search warrant to look for any other evidence of fraud. And guess what we'll find in your VCR storage cabinet. We'll find copies of movies made illegally, without the consent of the producer. Boom, another felony.

"After so much felonious conduct, we'll ask the IRS to audit you for the past seven years. I'm sure those bulldogs will find some problems with your taxes and charge you with tax evasion. Boom! We've got you on three felonies.

"Have you little boys ever heard the phrase 'three strikes and you're out?' Upon conviction of your third felony you're looking at life imprisonment with large men that have unnatural sexual urges." Skip let it all sink in and then said quietly, "Don't fuck with the feds."

101

Skip walked past the group, leaving Doug and Roger standing in shock with the others. For the first time in Doug's life, he was embarrassed to be a law enforcement officer.

Chapter 17

As Doug entered the courthouse's snackbar for a cup of coffee, he saw Barb Brandon sitting by herself in a corner studying a file. After he purchased his morning supply of caffeine, he approached Barb and said, "Good morning, counselor. Mind if I join you?"

Barb's green eyes lit up and she cheerfully replied, "Of course not, officer. But, I wouldn't want to ruin your reputation."

"I survived in the past. I guess I'll be OK this time," Doug said slyly as he sat down.

Barb looked into Doug's eyes and had a quick passion flashback that caused her to recross her legs. After a drink of her orange juice she said, "Well, we got the manatee trial coming up. Are you guys ready?"

"Of course we're ready, Barb. But let me ask you—why are we trying this case? It's open and shut," Doug asked. He looked at her fair complexion, naturally curly jet black hair touching her shoulders and the small freckles over her nose. She smiled knowingly, and he remembered her Irish blood that produced incredible streaks of passion whenever she drank whiskey.

Barb took another drink of her orange juice and said, "Doug, before I answer your question, let me tell you about this new case I just got retained on down in Miami; it'll help you understand.

"This elderly couple decides to commit suicide together because he has brain cancer and she has failing kidneys. So they make this plan to hang themselves together on the opposite ends of the same rope, and their own weight will kill each other. They had this favorite love-seat swing tied to a big branch on an oak tree in their yard. So they get this 12-foot piece of rope and tie a noose on each end and throw it over the branch where it falls down above the swing. They stand up on the swing and place the noose around each other's neck, kiss each other and jump.

"Well, guess what. As they're both hanging, the wife changes her mind. She gets her feet back on the swing and manages to loosen the noose from her neck. But, by the time she does this, her husband is dead. She calls 911 and the cops show up and charge her with first-degree murder. She hires me to defend her.

"Pretty wild shit, huh. Who knows what a jury will think of it. It just doesn't make sense. Kind of like this manatee case—it just doesn't make sense."

Barb smiled at Doug, gathered her files and stood up. She reached out, gently patted Doug on the shoulder and said, "Gotta run. When this trial's over, maybe we can go out for a drink."

Doug looked up at Barb's petite figure impressively displayed in a blue Armani suit and said, "Maybe."

Barb smiled and hurried off, obviously late to a court hearing. Doug enjoyed the view as she strutted away. He finished his cup of coffee and walked up to the third floor to meet with Roger.

When Doug walked into the State Attorney's Office, the receptionist said, "Mr. Shearer, we've been expecting you. Mr. Barklett wants to come out and walk with you to the post office."

Doug was confused but sat down and read a magazine until Roger made his way out. Roger met him and said, "I've been trying to get a little more exercise with this damn diet I'm on. I thought we could walk to the post office while we talked about the case."

"Sure," Doug replied as they headed for the stairs.

As they were walking out of the building, Barb crossed in front of them on the sidewalk, "Hello, guys. Have you found the real manatee killers yet? The courthouse gossip is that you guys have no motive for the trial."

Roger couldn't resist, "You haven't gotten my motion yet. I'm asking the court to force you to reveal who paid you to represent Buck. When I get that answer, I'll have my motive."

Barb's swagger was momentarily diminished until she realized Roger was pushing her buttons, "You almost had me, Roger. Fortunately, we have the attorney-client privilege to protect society from bulldog prosecutors that can't stand to lose."

Barb turned to go into the courthouse and Roger said, "Have a good day, counselor."

Barb smiled as she entered the courthouse, "Good bye, boys. I can't wait to see you in court."

As they walked towards the post office, Doug asked, "Why is she so cocky?"

Roger answered, "That's a little game she plays. She used to do it when she was a prosecutor. She tries to get the attorney on the other side worked up so he reveals something about his case to show he is smarter. She knows how to play egos like yo-yos."

It was a brisk spring day, and on the way back they stopped for a Diet Coke at the snack bar. They both took long drinks and relaxed.

Roger said, "Enough about work. How's Mary and Amanda?"

Doug looked weary and said, "Mary hasn't called for a while. Unfortunately, Amanda has been calling a lot. She wants...well...she wants me to move in. Says she wants some stability in her life. I don't know, though. It's fun to play house. But to move in? I don't know."

Roger laughed quietly and said, "Promise me something. Don't do anything until after this manatee trial. I'm already irritable with this damn diet. The last thing I need is to listen to your problems living with Amanda."

Doug took a deep breath and said quietly, "I promise."

105

Chapter 18

Doug awoke to his phone ringing. He glanced over at his clock and saw that it showed 4:50 a.m.

His telephone manners momentarily left him as he answered, "What is it?"

"Doug, Sgt. Busbee here. We've got another dead, headless manatee with a harpoon in his back. On its side, someone carved out, 'Fuck the feds.'   That official with Federal Fish and Wildlife, Skip Folly, found it this morning washed up on the beach, at the south entrance to Punta Blanca creek, in the mouth of the river. He was out in one of their boats looking for poachers. I've already ordered the dive boat to meet me there. Where should I meet you?"

Doug hesitated as he allowed his brain to slowly digest the news, "*Tarpon Point Marina* is the closest place. I'll drive there and meet you in an hour."

"10-4. See you in an hour."

Doug's anger jerked him from his sleepy state. He couldn't believe Buck and his co-conspirators would keep this killing spree going; especially a week before his trial. He also couldn't believe that Skip Folly was by himself in a government boat looking for poachers in the middle of the night. Doug felt his blood pressure increasing and could feel the veins pulsing in his neck. He started the coffee and sat down to relax as he thought about the new killing method.

It had been three weeks since the second set of killings and seven weeks since the first set. They had not been able to connect Buck to the second set. Doug knew it was imperative to connect Buck to this last killing or his lawyer would use it to show the real killer was still loose. Doug drank his coffee as he quickly dressed.

Fifty minutes later, Doug was parking his old Ford truck at *Tarpon Point Marina.* Doug walked down to the dock just as

Sgt. Busbee was pulling the sheriff's boat around the bend in the harbor. The sun was gradually brightening up the cloudless morning as the mosquitoes got in their last few bites before retiring to the mangroves. Sgt. Busbee eased the 25-foot boat up to the dock and Doug stepped aboard without the boat ever touching the dock.

"Have you found out anything else, Sgt.?"

"Well, maybe. We were getting the manatee ready to transport for a necropsy, so we cut the shaft of the harpoon sticking out of the manatee off. We looked at the handle and there is some blood there. It could be the manatee's blood or it could be the perp's. I gave it to the crime scene investigator and she is going to have a DNA test run on it."

Doug was relieved that he might have the potential to connect Buck to this crime. He rode out to the creek mouth to survey the scene and talk to the technicians at the scene. The manatee's right side was carved with letters approximately one-foot high spelling out, "Fuck the feds." Doug instantly thought of Skip Folly and his mentality. His next suggestion would be to outlaw combustible engines on all waters. No boats would be allowed except canoes, sailboats and small boats operated by electrical trolling motors. Doug felt nauseous and had to walk away from the smelly, decaying carcass.

Doug found Skip Folly making notes over by the undercover Federal Fish and Wildlife boat he had used. As Doug approached, Folly looked up and said, "Good morning, detective."

Doug looked at him warily, "You are one dedicated employee. It's hard to believe that you were by yourself, in strange waters, in the middle of the night and you just happened to find a dead manatee. Don't you think that is a little too convenient?"

Folly looked annoyed as he answered, "I'm just doing my job. May I suggest you do your job and find out who did this."

Doug forced himself to walk away from Folly, confused and irritated. After supervising the collection of evidence, the

107

transport of the carcass to Dr. Jones's office and the dive teams search for evidence or the missing heads, Sgt. Busbee returned Doug to the marina.

Doug was frustrated as he got off the boat and he asked, "What did they do with the damn heads?"

Sgt. Busbee shook his head negatively, "I have no idea. I do know that God will have a special place in hell for them, though."

Doug drove into downtown Ft. Myers and was waiting in the coffee shop for the State Attorney's office to open. Barb walked in with a glass of orange juice, saw Doug and walked over.

"Mind if I join you?"

"Not at all. I was just thinking about one of your clients, Buck Williams," Doug replied as he looked at something sticking to the bottom of Barb's shoe.

"That doesn't surprise me. I heard on the radio they found another beheaded manatee. So...do you know where Buck was last night? I assume you've been doing surveillance on him."

Doug looked at Barb's conceited smile and he began fuming. After the second set of killings, some people wanted to watch Buck 24/7, but he overruled it. He didn't think it was necessary or that Buck would actually be stupid enough to continue the killings. Barb had obviously heard through the courthouse gossip lines that there was no surveillance. Now he realized the blame game was going to start and he was going to be an easy target. On top of that, Barb was going to use the other killings to show that Buck wasn't responsible for the first.

Doug finally said, in his most polite voice, "No comment, counselor."

Doug rose up to leave and leaned over to whisper, "But there is something you should know, Barb. You have toilet paper stuck to the bottom of your shoes."

Doug walked towards the elevator as he savored embarrassing Barb. He knew that he was going to catch some flack from not watching Buck's movements at night. After going up to the third floor, Doug entered the state attorney's office and asked for Roger. The receptionist motioned for him to enter and go back to Roger's office. Moments later he entered and saw Roger pacing behind his desk looking out the window. When he heard Doug, he turned and said, "I was eating a banana for breakfast and drinking that fuckin' prune juice, when I hear this news flash, 'The manatee murders have continued. Local police and prosecutors appear impotent to stop the assault.'

"So, I switch channels and it's the lead story on every local channel. I switch to CNN and they're giving the history of the killings with the blood-red caption at the bottom, 'The Manatee Murders.' I walk into my office this morning and my boss is sitting in my chair. He wants me to find out who's behind this and charge them with every possible crime. He wants the maximum sentence and he wants our ass because we haven't stopped the killings."

Roger stopped his raving long enough to get his breath, "Any suggestions?"

Doug gave him a small smile, "Maybe. We found some blood on the handle of the harpoon found in the manatee. We've sent it off for a DNA analysis. If we can get a sample of Buck's blood, we might be able to match it."

Roger twirled around in delight, "That's some good news. I'll do an emergency motion asking the Court to order Buck to give us a blood sample and file it with the Court ASAP."

* * * *

The bailiff barked, "All rise, the honorable Brenda Lopez Tyler is presiding."

Judge Tyler sat down and waited a few seconds before she said, "Please be seated. I believe the state has an emergency motion that was filed yesterday. Mr. Barklett, you may proceed."

The reporters were on the edge of their chairs as Roger stood up. He cleared his throat and addressed his former lover, "Judge, in our motion we are asking for a sample of the defendant's blood to match with the human blood found on the harpoon that killed the most recent dead manatee. I've outlined in my motion the rules of procedure and caselaw that support my position."

"Mr. Barklett, I've read your motion and I'm inclined to agree with you. Ms. Brandon, do you have any objection to this motion?" Judge Tyler asked forcefully.

Barb was sitting next to Buck and she rose to address the Court in the packed courtroom, "Judge, this is not proper. It is an invasion of my client's privacy rights. There is no independent evidence connecting my client to this event. I would like to remind the Court that there are no witnesses that my client ever harmed a manatee. He was found in possession of a dead manatee, but that's not against the law."

Judge Tyler shifted in her chair and gave Barb an annoyed look, "Counselor, I don't understand how you can turn things around. I just..."

"Mrs. Judge, can I say something, please?" Buck blurted out.

Judge Tyler replied, "Sir, you need to talk to your attorney, before you address the court."

Buck quickly replied, "No, I don't judge. It's my blood on the damn harpoon."

There was an uproar in the audience while Judge Tyler and the lawyers had a look of shock on their face. Finally, Roger spoke up, "Your honor, the state appreciates the defendant's in-court confession to the crime. However, we need corroborating evidence to bolster the confession."

Judge Tyler looked menacingly at Buck and said, "The State's motion is granted. Your bond is revoked and you will be taken into custody to wait for trial next week. You will immediately give blood to a representative of the state. If you refuse, the state is given permission to forcibly retrieve a blood sample."

Chapter 19

Doug knew the trial date was rapidly approaching and a key piece of the puzzle was missing; all juries want to know the motive for the crime. Doug was pleased that the DNA from the blood on the harpoon matched Buck's blood, but it didn't give a motive. Doug called Roger and they agreed to meet at Doug's house after work to discuss the case. When Roger arrived in his old Buick Regal, Doug grabbed a beer and a Diet Coke for Roger, meeting him at the door. They walked out back towards the canal and sat on Doug's old picnic table by the seawall. The humidity was high, but the afternoon sea breeze cooled things down as the sun fell below the neighbor's roofline.

As Doug popped open his beer he asked, "Why do you behead a manatee and then hide the head? What good is a manatee head?"

Roger drank his Diet Coke and dismissed his craving for rum as he pondered a possible answer. Finally, he said, "A trophy. A mounted head like a tiger or lion. A collector wanted to add to his collection."

"Maybe. But why six heads and why a baby manatee? And why would you drag the carcasses to highly visible places so you know it would be discovered and outrage people?" Doug asked loudly.

"Good question. I guess we'll have to ask ole' Buck Williams when he takes the stand at his trial," Roger answered as he pictured the trial scene in his mind.

They finished their drinks in silence as they watched the sun set and felt the no-see-ums around their neck. Roger said, "One more thing before I go. I'm going to put forth possible theories of the case and I want you to play devil's advocate and poke holes in them."

"Go for it."

"First, imagine that there is a new market for manatee heads. A few years ago, commercial fisherman were taking the fins off of sharks and leaving them alive to swim in circles until they died. The same with mullet roe. The roe was worth more than the mullet meat. The poachers would take the roe and leave the rotting fish. What do you think?"

Doug thought for a minute and then said, "The problem with that is that everybody knew there was a market for shark fins or mullet roe because it was legal. There's no way there could ever be a legal market for manatees."

Roger answered, "Good point. How about my second theory—the manatee is a symbol to a group and they're trying to get publicity for their cause. How about that?"

Doug quickly answered, "If that was true, they would have contacted the press or issued some type of demand to stop the killing. No one has spoken out."

Roger threw up his hands, "Back to square one; no one knows why. You can bet Barb is going to say that a hundred times in front of the jury."

After the sky turned dark blue, a swarm of mosquitoes found them, and they had to run inside. The cool AC air produced goose bumps on their arms. After getting two fresh drinks, Doug pulled out his nautical charts and spread them on his dining room table. He found a red pen and circled where the manatee carcasses had been found.

Doug thought aloud, "Buck was driving an old mullet boat with a 60 Yamaha engine. Dragging a manatee through the water would slow the boat to a crawl. There's no way he could single-handedly trap three manatees, cut their heads off, dispose of the heads and drag the bodies to these locations between dark and when he was found at 2:00 a.m. He had to have people helping him.

"But what's the motive? An old commercial fisherman doesn't give a damn about manatee zones. It slows down the recreational flats boats with big engines. Commercial fisherman hate recreational fisherman because they got the net ban passed back in the mid-90's and put a lot of mullet fisherman out of business. They had to love it when all of these manatee zones screwed the recreational boater. Why would they kill a manatee?"

After an hour of debating the possible reasons of an old cracker commercial fisherman beheading a manatee, they were exhausted and no closer to an answer. Roger left to go home to a late supper with his wife, Betty.

Roger had met Betty through the personal ads. Her ad stated, "SWF, late 30's, petite blond, non-smoker, social drinker looking for financially and emotionally secure non-smoking, SWPM for a relationship. One night stand experts need not apply."

Roger was a very smart man who looked like an overweight bear. Betty had a small dose of brains but looked like a cross between an Olympic gymnast and a Barbie doll. However, opposites definitely attracted in their case, and they enjoyed their life together.

After Doug got a fresh beer, he turned on his country music and sat down at his computer. After logging on to the Internet, he typed in "manatee flesh" into his search engine and hit the enter button. After about 10 seconds, the screen showed 15 possible matches that were arranged in order of seniority of the site entries onto the web. The first 14 matches had to do with injuries to manatees and the damage to their bodies. The last match made Doug's head start pounding. It read as follows:

"Tokyo Daily News—Food Section: manatee brain latest craze"

Doug clicked on his mouse and the full article came up on his screen. He was shocked as he read that the most expensive men's clubs in Tokyo were serving manatee brain pureed into liquid as vanity drinks served in shot glasses. According to the reporter, the excellent taste was only a nice by-product; the real value was that all of the men that had drank the pureed manatee brain claimed it was much more potent than Viagara!

The article claimed that the demand for manatee brain was so high and the supply was so low, restaurants were paying $25,000 per manatee brain. The brain was pureed into a liquid and served in shot glasses for $1,000 per shot. Doug couldn't believe what he was reading; he couldn't picture an oriental man in Tokyo drinking a pureed manatee brain from Pine Island Sound.

Doug then remembered his history books. For centuries oriental men ate ground up elephant and rhino tusks. The rumor was that if a man consumed this ground up powder, his virility would grow tremendously. Doug then remembered recent local history in Florida. The reason there was a net ban passed is because of the indiscriminate netting for mullet. There was a huge demand for mullet roe in the orient because it was considered a delicacy and an aphrodisiac. The commercial fisherman would net the mullet and kill any sport fish that got caught in the net. There was so much netting that the breeding stock of all fish had declined rapidly.

Now manatee brain was the newest craze. Doug rubbed his eyes as he thought of poachers hunting manatees with harpoons in his home waters.

*   *   *   *

As Barb was sitting in the reception area of the Lee County Jail waiting for the correction officers to bring Buck Williams to the attorney visitation room, she thought back to the first time she met him after his arrest. She was allowed into the attorney visitation room to talk with him. She had expected a burly fisherman who was ready to fight the system that had imprisoned him. Instead, she found a tired old man sitting quietly in the corner observing his fellow inmates. It had been two days after his initial arrest and he looked pathetic. She had motioned for him to approach the window made of thick wire fence and introduced herself, "Hi, I'm Barb Brandon. I've been retained to represent you in this matter. How are you doing?"

114

Buck looked warily at her and said, "They didn't tell me they's gonna hire a female lawyer. You're awful pretty to be a lawyer; ya any good?"

Barb snapped, "I'm the best, Mr. Williams. We'll demand a speedy trial to get you in front of a jury as soon as possible. How does that sound?"

"Whatever you think, Mrs. Brandon."

"It's Ms. Brandon, I'm not married."

"I'm sorry, Ms. Brandon. I'm sure one day sumbody'll ask ya."

Barb smiled to herself as she replayed her first meeting with Buck. Buck had called her office at least a dozen times to talk about what was happening with the case.

The female correction officer working the front desk said through the speaker, "You can go up now, he's in visitation."

Barb got up and walked into the elevator. She was the only occupant and she looked at the four stainless steel walls with no controls. Barb had been riding in these elevators for over a dozen years, but they still made her nervous because there were no controls inside. You were totally at the mercy of the correction officer at the front desk operating the controls. There had been a number of mistakes over the years where mouthy, obnoxious defense lawyers ended up stuck in the elevators for hours because of sudden mechanical problems.

The elevator opened up on the fourth floor, and she walked out into the attorney visitation area. Buck was sitting in an adjacent room, on the other side of heavy plexiglass, patiently waiting for his pretty, unmarried, lawyer.

Barb sat down on the metal stool and spoke through the small holes in the plexiglass, "Good morning, Mr. Williams. How are you today?"

"I guess I'm fair to midllin'. They had some new syrup 'is mornin' for the pancakes; right tasty."

Barb didn't know whether to laugh or cry as she listened to Buck talk about his breakfast when he was looking at a possible sentence of thirty years in prison. She smiled politely and said,

"I'm glad you enjoyed your breakfast. I wanted to talk to you about your boat. It was an old wooden boat; do you know the towing capacity?"

Buck snickered to himself and said, "Well...since I made it twenty years ago, I don't think we did any towin' test."

Barb chided, "I can't believe you drove around in that thing at night with no lights."

"Let me tell ya sumthin' missy, my daddy had a boat like dat all his life and never sunk once. Remember, amateurs built the ark, but the Titanic was built by pros."

Buck started laughing to himself while Barb waited until he finished and then continued, "I guess you're right about that, Mr. Williams." She hesitated before finishing, "I wanted to make sure you knew your trial was coming up. The way the trial works is that we pick a jury and then have opening statements. The State puts on their witnesses first and then you can testify, if you want."

Buck looked intently at her, tapped his right index finger on the plexiglass and said firmly, "You can bet your purty sweet ass I'm gonna testify."

Chapter 20

Doug slowly awoke to his phone ringing, reached over and picked up the receiver, "Hello?"

"Good morning, Doug. I hope I didn't wake you up, but I wanted to talk," Amanda informed him in a very matter of fact voice.

Doug looked over at the clock and saw that it was 5:45 a.m. He realized he had only been asleep for five hours after a night of reviewing all the trial notes. He hesitated and asked "Is something wrong? Are you OK?"

"Well, I didn't sleep good last night; I missed you. You know, I...like having, you know, some one here at night, close and there to protect me if the boogyman comes for me," Amanda quietly purred.

There was silence on the line, and then Amanda continued in a stronger voice, "So I was feeling tired and lonely when I walked out to get the morning paper. Then I see the damn headline in the paper! Have you seen it yet?"

Doug stammered, "No, I haven't seen it yet."

"Well you should like it," Amanda hissed sarcastically. She hesitated and her voice cracked as she continued, "Doug I need stability in my life. I desperately want you in my life but if...if you don't want me, I need to look out for myself. Trevor wants me to move back to Sarasota and marry him—without a prenuptial."

Doug looked at the clock and it read 5:47 a.m. He thought it was not polite for so much to be thrown at a man in two minutes when jarred out of a perfectly good sleep. He mumbled, "I don't know what to say."

"I don't either Doug, but I need to do something. It's Tuesday. He wants me to go with him to a golf tournament on Saturday," Amanda let her predicament sink in and continued,

117

"You have until Friday at 6:00 p.m. to decide if you want me in your life or not. Oh, and by the way, enjoy your paper."

Amanda hung up, and Doug had to scratch his head and recreate what had just happened. He was still trying to figure it out as he turned on the lights, walked out his front door and down his driveway. There was a sparse early morning fog spread throughout Doug's neighborhood. Three driveways down he could see a family of raccoons scavenging through the neighbor's trash bags out for pickup. He grabbed his paper, walked back inside and sat down at his dining room table, spreading it out.

The bold headlines read, *Ex-lovers litigate Manatee Murders.*

Doug saw his picture next to Barb Brandon's. Below it was Roger Barklett's picture next to Judge Tyler's. The two page article detailed Doug's history with Barb Brandon and how she and Judge Tyler had bid against each other at the charity auction. The article also detailed Roger's romance with Judge Tyler and how he dumped her after she lost sight in her right eye. There was a separate article detailing the attack on Judge Tyler while she had Lasik eye surgery. There was a color picture of her before the attack and one after the attack, showing her lavender patch.

There was a separate interview with George Steinworth of *Save Our Seacows* about the relationships. He predictably steered away from the dating habits of the parties to the manatee. He listed different statistics about the manatee and how they were endangered. His last quote of the article was, "The courts are the conscience of the community. We need the maximum punishment as a strong detriment to others. The local cracker fishermen are nothing but lawless animals that are worse than trailer trash."

The phone rang as Doug finished reading the paper and he answered, "Hello."

"Did you see the paper yet?" Roger yelled into his phone.

"Yeah, I saw it. I didn't realize what a heartless bastard you were."

Roger chuckled and said sarcastically, "Oh, you think that's funny? Can you imagine what all of our potential jurors are thinking as they read the paper this morning?"

Doug considered the dilemma and said, "Well at least the prosecutor and defense lawyer are equally trashed by the article, so maybe the jurors won't care."

"Yeah, but you expect that kind of shit from defense lawyers," Roger quipped.

Doug laughed and said, "Well, what time do we meet in the war room to get everything ready to go?"

"Nine o'clock. I'll see you then," Roger said and hung up.

The war room was the main conference room at the State Attorney's Office that Roger had taken over for all of the exhibits and material for the trial. Along the back wall were 2' by 4' pictures of the dead manatees where they were found. Next to them were 4' by 8' charts of the islands and waters of Pine Island Sound where the carcasses were found. On the opposite side of the room were 2' by 4' pictures of Buck Willliam's boat and the chainsaw. On the large oval table in the middle were packets for the jurors that showed a summary of the DNA evidence and smaller pictures of the exhibits.

On the drive into downtown Ft. Myers, Doug called Amanda at home on his cell phone. After three rings she picked up and said, "Well, did you like the article?"

Doug stammered, "How did you know it was me?"

Amanda acted bored and said, "I have caller ID and I screen my calls. I almost didn't pick up."

Doug quickly downshifted his tone from confrontational to apologetic and said, "I'm sorry about that article; it was a long time ago. I'm sorry if it hurt your feelings."

Amanda's shield started to melt and she said, "It's O.K. It was just a bit much for me this morning before I had my coffee and cigarette."

Doug waited for few seconds and then asked, "Can I come over tonight?"

Amanda quickly answered, "Of course. I'll go shopping and we can eat in tonight."

Doug smiled and said, "I'll be over about seven."

For the rest of the ride, Doug thought of how much fun it was to make up after a fight with Amanda. He decided to avoid the looming decision over his future with her. When Doug arrived at the war room, Roger was already at work cross-checking his witnesses' travel itineraries and hotel registrations with his secretary. Doug poured a cup of coffee as Roger finished up and sat down. When Roger's secretary walked out of the war room, Doug said, "I've got something to tell you. I don't think you're gonna like it."

Roger turned sharply and glared at Doug, "I don't need any problems. The biggest trial of my life starts tomorrow, and I've got enough shit to deal with. What is it?"

Doug threw his hands up in front of him and said "Slow down, big guy. It doesn't affect the proof at trial, but it might go to the motive of Buck Williams if he decides to testify."

Roger sat down, took a deep breath and said, "Let's hear it."

Doug proceeded to tell Roger about his discovery of pureed manatee brain as a delicacy in Tokyo and the side effect of outperforming Viagara. Roger's face tightened and looked instantly tired as he said, "Are you telling me that there is a $25,000 bounty on every manatee in Lee County?"

Doug scratched his head as he moved it back and forth while he said, "I don't know what to think."

Roger looked down and kept mumbling, "More beheaded manatees. More manatee murders."

After a few minutes of silence, Roger got up and walked to the window. Doug decided to try to bring his friend back from his depression and said, "It looks like you've been losing some weight."

Roger slowly shook his head up and down as his face lightened up, "Yeah, a little bit. About 15 pounds. At least I'm not popping buttons off my shirt."

Doug's beeper went off, and he looked down for the number. His stomach turned as he realized Mary had paged him. He hadn't talked to her for almost a week and now the trial was starting tomorrow. He decided to call her back and buy some time.

Mary answered, "Oh my god! You actually returned a page. How did I get so lucky?"

Doug said, "I'm sorry. There's a lot going on with this trial. We start picking a jury tomorrow morning, and we should be done in two days. After that I promise to make it up to you."

There was silence on the other end as Mary fumed. She finally said, "Doug, do whatever makes you happy. I hope your crime files keep you warm at night."

Mary hung up, and Doug looked up at Roger who was smiling. Roger said, "You single guys have all the fun."

"Yeah, right."

"We've got to make a decision about that Tokyo news article. Do we bring it up a trial? How can we connect it to Buck and the dead manatees?"

Doug answered, "I've made some calls. The article came out three weeks ago in Tokyo. The editors at the paper don't want to cooperate and the cops over there laughed at me when I asked for help. So, there's no way to prove where these alleged manatee brains came from."

Roger considered the problems and said, "We would look foolish in front of the jury and Barb would ask for a mistrial. She would argue to the judge that we were trying to inflame the jury with evidence that can't be connected to Buck. I don't think Judge Tyler will cut us any breaks. However, we could keep it in our back pocket in case Buck testifies at trial. We might be able to use it for impeachment."

The rest of the day Doug and Roger made sure everything was ready for trial. Finally they left the war room at 6:30 p.m.

confident they were going to convict Buck Williams of all charges.

Doug arrived at Amanda's condo promptly at seven. She greeted him in a leopard skin lingere, and Doug momentarily forgot everything about the manatee case. After a dinner of Chicken Marsala and spinach salad they retired to the balcony and looked over the dark Caloosahatchee River below them. Amanda had left a bottle of champagne and glasses chilled in an ice bucket. Doug opened the bottle and they drank it while watching the brightly lit boats travel up and down the river at a slow speed.

As the nearly full moon rose over the horizon, Amanda stepped forward and gently kissed Doug. He felt pleasure flowing through his veins, but he couldn't get Amanda's ultimatum out of his mind. They retired to Amanda's bedroom and gently made love. For the first time in his life, Doug's mind was not overwhelmed by Amanda's sexual prowess. He couldn't help but wonder if he could trust this beautiful woman who had crushed his heart years before. After the pleasurable session was over, they rested on the sweaty silk sheets. Doug was totally relaxed and drifting fast towards a well-needed sleep. The instant before his brain surrendered to slumber, he heard the fateful words, "Whatcha thinkin'?"

Chapter 21

Roger was looking at his different suits, deciding which one would have the best first impression on the jury, when his wife walked into the bedroom carrying him a cup of coffee. Roger smiled, took the cup and asked, "Which suit for the first day—somber black or believable blue?"

Betty contemplated the choice and said, "Believable blue looks better on you. Besides, you can wear more colorful ties with the blue."

Roger pulled out the blue suit and then took a sip of coffee. Betty was looking through his ties and said, "Here's the perfect one." She held up a solid red tie and continued, "The paper has an article about the *Save Our Seacows* club members all wearing red shirts to court today to show their support. This red one will make them happy and you can wear a white shirt to show your red, white and blue patriotism for the jury. I wonder if...Judge Tyler likes red?"

Roger snapped his head around and said, "All right, enough of the Judge Tyler jokes."

Betty laughed as she left the room and said, "Is it true that red is her favorite color for bras?"

Roger's temper started to fester as he thought of the recent pre-trial publicity about his prior relationship with Judge Tyler when he was single. He convinced himself that potential jurors would think it was funny and not be bothered by it. He was concerned about how Judge Tyler would react about having her dirty laundry aired in public. The more he considered it, the more he realized he was going to have to be especially respectful to her in public.

After Roger dressed, he was thrilled that his red-tagged suit was not tight and the collar of his shirt buttoned easily. The fifteen pounds he had lost in the past two weeks was showing.

This boost of confidence is exactly what Roger needed as he walked out to his car.

He arrived early at the courthouse and headed up to the war room near his office. His secretary had arrived early and already had the coffee brewing. Roger thanked her as he poured his cup full. Roger never ate breakfast on trial days. His nerves always produced an unsettled stomach that didn't mix well with eggs and bacon. He sat down and looked over his checklist for the exhibits and all of his notes. His first sip of the coffee burnt his lip and he jerked away from the cup. He sat the hot cup down and walked over to the window, looking out over the front entrance to the courthouse.

The protesters from *Save Our Seacows* were already organizing and passing out signs. Roger could see that George Steinworth was in the middle of the group and pointing to different areas. The first sign was a white poster board with red letters that read A Life for a life! Life in prison for the manatee murderer! A second sign was on yellow poster board with green letters that read STOP THE SLAUGHTER! SAVE OUR SEACOWS!

All of the workers in the courthouse and potential jurors had to walk the gantlet of signs thrust in their face by the *Save Our Seacows* protesters. Roger sat back down and carefully sipped his coffee. He was loading up his trial cart to move all of the exhibits and files to the courtroom when Doug walked in. Roger stacked up his notes and asked, "Ready for the big day?"

Doug smiled and nodded, "Oh, yeah. I can't wait 'til we convict Buck and have this show over. I can't wait to go back to normal crimes with humans."

Doug held the door open wide as Roger pushed his loaded cart out of the war room. Doug walked in front of him and cleared all of the pulled back chairs and partially open doors until they reached the elevator. Doug hit the up button and a moment later an elevator opened. Barb Brandon, dressed in her own believable blue suit, was standing in the back with her own trial cart. After everyone put on a forced smile, Doug asked, "Is there room for us?"

Barb smiled, "Of course. Especially since Roger has lost weight. Trying to look good for the cameras… or maybe an old girlfriend?"

Roger smiled, pushed his cart into the elevator and said, "Ouch, first blood goes to the Irish vixen dressed in Italian Armani."

Doug looked at a man's brown suit folded over the top of Barb's cart and asked, "So are you going to try to dress up Buck? Kinda like putting perfume on a skunk."

Barb answered, "Of course. No jury could give a man a fair trial dressed in an orange jumpsuit, labeled in bold, white letters *LEE COUNTY JAIL* and white sandals."

Roger quipped, "Especially with two eyewitnesses and DNA evidence."

Barb snorted and cut her eyes to Roger as the elevator doors opened on the fifth floor. The bright lights from the TV cameras quickly turned on as three reporters rushed forward towards Barb and one asked, "How can your client be not guilty when they found him with one of the murdered manatees?"

The second reporter asked, "Will Mr. Williams testify?"

The third reporter quickly chimed in, "Is your client involved in voodoo?"

Barb stopped, raised her hands in front of her and said, "There is a voodoo issue in this case." Barb turned and looked at Roger as she continued, "Mr. Barklett just told me he is bringing a high priestess as an expert witness. You really should talk to him."

The reporters all became instantly stimulated by the new lead and rushed towards Roger. The loud questions in the small hallway in front of the elevators with the bright, hot camera lights were very annoying. Barb smiled coyly and waived as she walked towards courtroom "B" unmolested by the ravenous reporters.

There was a reason for Barb's white lie. She wanted to be the first to the courtroom. Courtroom "B" had a lighter look than traditional courtrooms. The dark wood favored in older courthouses was replaced with a white pine. To the right of the judge's bench an American flag was hanging from a polished brass holder. To the left a Florida flag matched. The witness stand was to the right of the judge, the clerk's station to the left. The jury box was to the right of the witness stand and turned at an angle to allow for a clear view of the witness and the judge. Traditionally, prosecutors sat at the counsel table closest to the jury box. Most of the time defense lawyers abided by the custom and sat at the other table. Barb decided she was going to try to upset Roger's comfort level by taking the counsel table closest to the jury box.

Barb was the only person in the courtroom as she unloaded her cart. By the time Roger and Doug had made it through the reporter's roadblock and entered the courtroom, she was sitting down, relaxed. The reporters stayed at the elevators trying to get a good quote from Buck's family or Steinworth and his *SOS* supporters.

"What the hell are you doing at my table?" an annoyed Roger yelled.

"Last night I checked the criminal rules of procedure and I didn't notice anything about this table being the prosecutor's table. Do you have a cite?" Barb asked sweetly.

"Yeah, I have a cite—it's called Judge Tyler's law. We'll let her decide," Roger shot back.

"Well, you should know whether she likes a prosecutor from the left or right side," Barb remarked.

Roger simmered as Doug started to unload the cart. The door back to the judge's chambers opened and Sgt. Chuck Percersi walked in. Sgt. Percersi was the head bailiff for the sheriff's office. He had worked twenty years as a street cop in Chicago and retired to Ft. Myers. After two years of hacking up turf on the area golf courses, he decided to have a second career as a bailiff. He started out in small claims court keeping warring

126

neighbors from strangling each other. His muscular 250 pounds was proportionately spread out on his 6'2'' frame. His salt and pepper gray hair combined with his bushy mustache produced an imposing authority figure with a uniform and gun. Over the past nine years, Sgt. Percersi had worked his way up the ranks to become the lead officer in the bailiff's division.

His hair was slicked back and after his divorce three years ago, considered himself available for every woman from 18-60. Even though eighty percent of the women he propositioned turned him down, Sgt. Percersi kept busy with the other twenty percent. He went to a tanning salon two nights a week and the beach on the weekends. Judge Tyler had requested that he be transferred to her court a year ago. Since then, Judge Tyler had a standing order filed that Sgt. Percersi be assigned to her courtroom until further notice. The rumor mill had produced many stories about the unusual arrangement.

"So what's all tha noiz' I hear? Can't youz two get along? Judge Tyler told me I's gonna hav' ta keep a tight rope on youz two," Sgt. Percersi belted out.

Barb smiled and said in her best maiden-in-distress voice, "Sgt. these two guys are pickin' on me. Can you help?"

Sgt. Percersi puffed out his chest and said, "Miss Brandon, I'll do whatever you want."

Barb said quietly, "I got here first and set my things on this table and they want it."

Sgt. Percersi was confused with this overwhelming problem and stammered, "Uh, geez, I don't know, Miss Brandon. That's the prosecutor's table. I gotta ask the judge."

Roger said, "Sgt. Percersi, before you ask the judge, maybe you should fix your zipper."

Sgt. Percersi looked down in embarrassment, grabbed his zipper and said, "Oh, shit! I can't believe I did that. I hope Johnson and the ugly twins are OK."

Sgt. Percersi laughed at his own joke as he opened the door and went back to chambers. Doug and Roger laughed at Sgt. Percersi's warped sense of humor and noticed Barb's uneasy silence. Roger asked, "What's the matter, Barb? Couldn't you put the bailiff under your spell?"

"Give me a break, guys."

Doug piped up, "Barb, so how do you think the judge will rule on this first issue. She hates both you and Roger. What a dilemma for her."

A few seconds later, Sgt. Percersi entered and announced in a loud voice, "All rise, Judge Brenda Lopez Tyler is presiding." Judge Tyler entered the courtroom, formally dressed in her black judicial gown, sat down in her over-stuffed burgundy chair and said, "Please, be seated."

Doug thought it was a surreal scene for a formal introduction—no one in the courtroom but the two lawyers for the opposite side, himself and the bailiff. Doug decided that Judge Tyler was setting the tone for the trial.

Judge Tyler looked at her former lover and then her former rival for Doug's affections, while ignoring Doug, and said, "Children, children, children. Can't we agree on anything? Ms. Brandon it's my custom in this courtroom that the prosecutor sits at that table. Please change places when we recess. I'll be back on the bench at 8:30 a.m. sharp."

Judge Tyler stood up and Sgt. Percersi said, "All rise." When Judge Tyler went back into chambers her loyal bailiff followed and, as he shut the door, said, "Youz can sit down, now."

Doug and Roger loaded their cart in silence as Barb did the same. Doug and Roger wheeled their cart over to their reclaimed table and walked out of the courtroom to avoid Barb's silence.

As they stood at the window looking out towards the U.S. 41 overpass, Doug said, "Well, that was fun."

Roger nodded, "She was sending a very stern message to both of us. This isn't going to be a pleasant trial."

Doug looked at his watch and said, "It's 8:05 a.m.; only a few more minutes to showtime."

They heard a squeaky wheel and looked down the hall at the clerk wheeling her own trial cart to the courtroom. The clerk passed them and said hello as she entered the courtroom. They looked back down the hall and saw Mrs. Ruth Burnsmith huffing down the hall with her court reporting equipment. Burnsmith was in her fifties and looked like a retired school marm. Her gray hair was pulled back in a tight bun. She wore no makeup and only a pale pink shade of lipstick. She was the consummate perfectionist and a neat freak. Her transcripts were always 100% accurate and prepared on time.

Her neatness was legendary. Her routine was the same every time she entered a courtroom. She would take a small bottle of disinfectant out of her purse and spray the vinyl court reporter's chair that stayed in the courtrooms. She would wipe it off with papertowel and then do the same to the sidebar where she would have to move her machine and lean if the judge called the parties forward. All of the judges put up with her quirky habits because of her excellent work. Her husband had died ten years before, and one of the most tasteless jokes in the courthouse was, "Why did Mrs. Burnsmith's husband die at forty?" The answer was, "because he wanted to."

Doug and Roger stood by the window as Mrs. Burnsmith went into the courtroom and sanitized her corner of the world. After a few minutes of idle chatter, Doug and Roger entered the courtroom and unpacked their cart on the prosecutor's table. Sgt. Percerci's assistant bailiff for the day was Corporal Isabella "Nails" Sanchez. Cpl. Sanchez was a mother of two in her mid-thirties. She wore very little makeup or jewelry, but she enjoyed having her long nails manicured weekly and painted different colors. One week they would be a glittery blue and the following week a fluorescent orange. Cpl. Sanchez was a by-the-book bailiff and she constantly had to remind Sgt. Percersi of the proper procedure whenever they worked together.

Cpl. Sanchez approached Doug and said, "Good morning, detective. How're you this morning?"

Doug looked at her nails and was shocked by her rather boring candy apple red color as he said, "I'm doing great. How are the kids?"

Cpl. Sanchez beamed as she quickly replied, "Both made the honor role last month. I hope they keep it up."

Doug looked around the courtroom for Barb and asked, "Where's Miss Brandon?"

Cpl. Sanchez nodded towards the side door in the courtroom and said, "I opened up the holding cell for her. She was taking the defendant his street clothes for trial."

The courtroom door opened and the red shirts of the *Save Our Seacows* members poured in. Similar to the seating arrangements at a wedding, they filled all of the seats behind the prosecutor's table except for the first two rows reserved for jurors. After they got situated, Buck Williams' family members filtered in and sat behind the defense table. Finally, Peter Hoyem and other members of the media filled in the remaining open chairs in anticipation of day one of the trial.

At 8:30 a.m. sharp, the chambers door to the courtroom opened as Sgt. Percersi entered and announced, "All rise, the Honorable Brenda Lopez Tyler is presiding over this court."

Judge Tyler entered the courtroom in her black robe and lavender patch over her right eye. She stepped up to the bench, sat down, took a breath and said, "You may be seated."

There was a momentary rise in the noise level as everyone sat down and got comfortable. The side door to the courtroom opened and Barb hurried back to her seat, still holding Buck's brown suit. Judge Tyler stared at her as she walked back to her table and finally said, "It's so nice of you to join us this morning, Miss Brandon. I hope we didn't start too early for you."

"I apologize your Honor. I was in the holding cell with my client and we... have a little problem."

"Miss Brandon, *we* don't have a problem. *You* may have a problem, but *we* don't have any problems," Judge Tyler bellowed.

Barb took a deep breath as members of *Save Our Seacows* snickered. She looked at Judge Tyler and said in her most professional voice, "I apologize, your Honor. It is my problem.

However, it concerns the defendant's right to a fair trial. May I be heard?"

Judge Tyler replied curtly, "Yes, you may. But we need your client first. Sgt. Percersi, please bring out the defendant."

Sgt. Percersi and Cpl. Sanchez went back to the holding cell and returned a few seconds later with Buck Williams between them. Buck was wearing his orange jumpsuit and white sandals. As he slowly walked to the defense table, Doug thought he looked very sickly and pale. As Buck sat down, he nodded to his family sitting behind him. Baylee had to wipe tears away with a very old homemade handkerchief.

Judge Tyler looked sternly at Barb and said, "You may proceed."

Barb said, "Your honor, the defendant's family brought me a suit for Mr. Williams to wear today in front of the jury. He now tells me that he doesn't want to wear the suit. I've tried to explain to him why this is needed, but he doesn't want to wear it."

Judge Tyler turned her glare towards Buck and said, "Sir, your lawyer and your family want you to wear street clothes in front of the jury. I don't care what you do. However, I should advise you that the jury might form a bad opinion of you wearing the jail's jumpsuit. It's your choice."

Buck looked down at his jumpsuit and then at the brown suit spread out on the table. He slowly nodded his head up and down as he said, "Judge, I reckon' I'll just wear this orange suit. I ain't got nothin' ta hide."

Judge Tyler banged her gavel and said, "So be it. Sgt. Percersi bring in the jury."

The jury clerk had brought up 30 prospective jurors and had them standing outside the courtroom, waiting on the Judge. Sgt. Percersi walked to the back of the courtroom, opened the door and motioned for the jurors to come in. They sat down in the first two rows as the clerk prepared to randomly call them to the jury box. After the jury box was filled with 12 prospective jurors, Judge Tyler addressed them, "Good morning, ladies and

131

gentlemen. Today we have a criminal trial for you. It's the case of State of Florida vs. Buck Williams. The defendant has been accused of three counts of manatee harassment."

There was a noticeable stir among the jurors. Some were smiling, some were angry and some confused by the excitement of their fellow jurors.

It took all morning for the six-member jury to be selected and sworn in. Judge Tyler dismissed them for lunch and instructed them to be back at one o'clock sharp for opening statements. Doug and Roger spent the lunch hour in the war room eating peanuts and drinking diet Cokes while debating what to include in the opening statement. At 12:55 p.m. they headed back to courtroom "B" and the eager jury.

At 1:00 p.m. the door to chambers opened as Sgt. Percersi announced, "All rise, the Honorable Judge Brenda Lopez Tyler is presiding."

Judge Tyler sat down and announced, "Everyone please be seated. Ladies and Gentleman, Mr. Roger Barklett will give the opening statement for the state."

Roger stood up, walked over to the podium, paused and then said in a polite voice, "Good afternoon, ladies and gentlemen. This is not going to be a pleasant case. You will hear about the killing of three manatees. You will hear about and see pictures of headless manatees. You will see where these beheaded manatees were found.

"And...you will also hear that...this man," Roger pointed towards Buck and continued in a louder voice, "was found leaving a headless manatee carcass when the police showed up. You will hear that in his boat the police found a chainsaw. On this chainsaw, there was manatee flesh from the three dead manatees. This will be proven by DNA evidence.

"After all of the evidence is presented, we'll ask you to return guilty verdicts on all three counts. Thank you for your attention."

As Roger walked back to his table, Judge Tyler looked at Barb and asked, "Does the defense wish to make an opening statement?"

Barb stood and answered quickly, "Yes, your honor." She walked to the podium and continued, "Ladies and Gentlemen of the jury, thank you for your attention here today. Mr. Williams is not guilty of manatee harassment. He is guilty of being at a crime scene when the police showed up. You will not hear any witness say they observed Buck touching any manatees that were alive. One of the elements the state has to prove, beyond a reasonable doubt, is that the manatees were alive when they was harassed by Mr. Williams."

The members of *Save Our Seacows* club had heard enough and they started snorting through their nose and rolling their eyes. Judge Tyler banged her gavel and yelled, "Order! Order! There'll be no talking in my courtroom." She looked at Barb and said, "You may continue Ms. Brandon."

Barb looked back at the jury and pleaded, "Please keep an open mind until you hear all the evidence." She walked back and sat down next to Buck, patting his hand.

"Mr. Barklett, call your first witness."

Roger stood up and said, "The state calls Deputy Gary Burns."

The door to the witness room opened and a uniformed deputy walked towards the clerk. The clerk stood up and said, "Please raise your right hand. Do you swear or affirm that everything you say in this courtroom is true?"

Deputy Burns firmly said, "I do."

Deputy Burns was in his late thirties and had made a decision to wear his belt below his abundant belly. Dep. Burns huffed his way to the witness stand and sat down.

"Deputy Burns please tell us how long you've been with the sheriff's office?

"Let's see, I started as a corrections officer after I got out of the Army. I did that for two years and then I went on the road

133

for eight years. I've been on the marine patrol unit for 18 months now."

"Dep. Burns, where were you working on the night of March 2nd this year?

"Oh, let's see. My partner and I picked up the boat from the substation at Pineland Marina. We had run over to Barnacle Phil's on Upper Captiva, when we got a message from dispatch. They'd received a phone call about illegal netting in the Roosevelt Channel, behind 'Tween Waters. So, we went there as fast as possible. We didn't use a blue light 'cause we were tryin' to sneak up on 'em."

"What did you see when you arrived on the scene?"

"Well, we was comin' up real slow in the channel. There were a few anchored sailboats and yachts just off the channel so we didn't have a clear line of sight. Then as we passed a group of anchored boats, we get another call from dispatch. Somebody else was complaining about illegal netting in the same place. About another 300 yards I see the defendant's unlit boat as he attempted to flee. After we turned on our lights, we saw a splash next to the Defendant's boat. We run up to it and saw the manatee carcass. We then gave chase until we apprehended the defendant."

"What did you see in the defendant's boat?"

"There was a bunch of wet rope in the bottom of the boat and a bloody chainsaw. We secured the boat and arrested the defendant. I took the chainsaw into evidence and sent off for a DNA analysis on the flesh that was on the blades. It matched all three dead manatees."

Roger looked at Judge Tyler and said, "No further questions."

Judge Tyler looked at Barb and said, "You may inquire."

"Deputy, did you see my client tie up a manatee?"

"Well, no I didn't. I just saw him with it after he killed it."

"Objection, non-responsive," Barb shouted.

"Overruled, move along, Miss Brandon."

Barb looked at the deputy and asked in a quieter tone, "Deputy, how did my elderly client catch a manatee, hold it down and chop off his head with a loud chainsaw?"

Dep. Burns scratched his head and said, "I don't know. Good question."

Barb looked at Roger and smiled, "No further questions."

As Dep. Burns stepped down from the witness stand, Judge Tyler said, "Call your next witness."

"The state calls Sgt. Sally Gardner."

The witness room door opened and Sgt. Gardner walked towards the clerk and was sworn in. After she sat down in the witness chair, Roger asked, "Please state your name and where you work."

"My name is Sally Gardner and I work for the Lee county sheriff's office as a crime scene investigator."

"Could you tell the jury what crime scene you were working on March 2nd of this year?"

"Well, actually there were four crime scenes. The manatees were found at three separate locations and the defendant was found at a fourth location."

"Sgt. Gardner, please explain what you did at each scene."

"The first scene was where the defendant was arrested. We secured all of the evidence in the boat. There was a bloody chain saw with some type of flesh on it. After another deputy took the tissue samples for DNA evidence, we did a fingerprint analysis. The only fingerprints on the chainsaw were the defendant's.

"We put out an anchor on the boat and waited on the divers. Once the divers came to the scene we had them dive near the boat to look for weapons and...the heads from the manatees."

Roger asked Sgt. Gardner about the other crime scenes and her investigation. There were no weapons or manatee heads recovered at any of the scenes. After Roger finished his direct examination, Barb approached the podium for cross-examination and asked, "Did the chainsaw kill the manatees?"

"I'm not sure. There was a necropsy done by a veterinarian; I'm not qualified to give a cause of death."

135

"Let me ask it another way. Is there any evidence, at any of the crime scenes, that proves the manatees were alive at the time their heads were cut off?"

Sgt. Gardner hesitated and said, "I don't know. We were never trained with manatees."

There were a few snickers from Buck's family that were quickly silenced by the one-eyed stare of Judge Tyler. Buck sat back in his chair and glared at the *Save Our Seacows* members.

"Is it possible the manatees were already dead when the heads were severed?"

"Anything is possible."

Barb looked at the jury and then Judge Tyler as she said, "No further questions."

As Sgt. Gardner walked out of the courtroom, Roger stood up and said, "The state calls Dr. Gregory Jones."

The door to the witness room opened and a gray-haired, bespeckled man in a blue seersucker suit entered. He walked quickly over to the clerk and raised his hand to be sworn in, as he had many times before. He stepped up to the witness stand, sat down in the witness chair, looked over at Judge Tyler and nodded.

Roger began his questioning, "Doctor, please tell the jury about your training."

Dr. Jones sat back in his chair and looked at the jury as he said, "I graduated from the University of Florida and then went to Georgia Southern to get my veterinarian degree. I did my internship at a clinic in Miami. For the past 15 years I have run my own clinic in Naples."

"Dr. Jones, on or about March 2nd of this year, did you have an opportunity to do a necropsy on three manatees?"

"Yes, I did."

"Could you tell the jury what you found?"

"It was a very unusual situation because all of the manatees had their heads cut off. It was impossible to tell the exact cause of death. All of the internal organs appeared to be in working order before some unnatural event caused the deaths. However,

136

the time of death was 12-14 hours before my exam for two of the manatees and 24-36 hours on the third."

"Dr. Jones, can you tell if the manatees were alive at the time they were beheaded?"

Dr. Jones took a deep breath and considered his answer. He finally said, "I can't give a definitive 'yes' or 'no.' But I can give you some guidance. I can tell the manatees heads were removed very close to the times of death and in fact, it might well have caused the death. The clotting of the blood throughout the rest of the body shows that the manatees were alive and healthy until a traumatic event, such as a beating with a heavy object, or cutting with a chainsaw or shooting with a gun caused the brain to quit functioning and a large quantity of blood poured our of the wound to the head. Because we don't have the heads, it's impossible to give the exact cause of death."

"Dr. Jones, did you do the necropsy on the second set of killings?"

"Objection, relevance," Barb barked as she stood up.

Judge Tyler raised her hands, "Counselors, please approach sidebar."

Ms. Burnsmith quickly left her seat and reached her sanitized area before anyone could take her place at sidebar.

After Barb and Roger reached sidebar, Judge Tyler whispered, "Mr. Barklett, where are you going with this? The defendant has not been charged with any other manatee killings. How is this relevant?"

Roger took a deep breath, "Judge, it's relevant to show the modus operandi between the two killings are the same because the heads are cut off."

Barb loudly whispered, "Judge, there were no darts on the first set of killings. This is extremely prejudicial."

Judge Tyler slowly scratched her lavender eye patch and said, "I'm going to allow it. Please continue."

Roger returned to the podium and asked, "Dr. Jones, did you do the necropsy on the second set of killings?"

"Yes, I did."

"Could you tell the jury what you found?"

"I found two adult manatees that had been killed by darts. These darts are commercial grade commonly used by veterinarians, park rangers and zoologist throughout the world. However, these darts had been altered. Cyanide had been inserted in the darts after the tranquilizer fluid had been removed. Someone was well trained; I'm quite certain the manatees were dead within 30 seconds."

"Thank you Dr. Jones, I don't have any other questions," Roger said.

Barb approached the podium and asked, "Dr. Jones, did you find any fiberglass fragments in the manatees?"

Dr. Jones nodded his head up and down as he answered, "Yes. Two of the manatees had large trauma areas to the side of the animal, near the ribs. A closer examination showed that there were shards of fiberglass in this trauma area."

"Dr. Jones, isn't it true that these shards of fiberglass were somehow scraped into the manatee sides within 24 hours of their death?"

"Yes, that's true. We could tell that no scabs had formed around the abrasions and where the shards entered the body. This is proof that the wounds were done very close to the time of death."

"Dr. Jones, isn't it true that you ran tests of these fiberglass shards to try to determine their origin?"

"Yes, that's true. But we couldn't prove which boat it came from."

"Dr. Jones, isn't it true that you could tell by the polymer mix in the fiberglass that it was manufactured in the past five years."

"Yes, that's true."

"Could a twenty-year old wooden fishing boat have caused these fiberglass shards?"

"No, they could not."

Dr. Jones, when you examined the baby manatee, didn't it have a hole in the middle of the carcass where it was impaled on a mangrove branch?"

"Yes, that's true."

"Dr. Jones, didn't you note in your report that the hole in the carcass was made by an extremely sharp knife that produced acute entry and exit wounds?"

"Yes, that's true. The hole in the body had been cut with a very sharp knife that produced a circular type wound. There was no torn flesh or muscles. To me, that indicated a large knife, possibly commercial grade, was used to slice through the flesh in a very efficient manner."

"Dr. Jones, isn't it true that there was no such knife found in Buck Williams' boat?"

"According to the police reports, there was no such knife found."

"Dr. Jones, didn't you also do the necropsy on the third set of killings?"

Roger stood up, "Objection, relevance."

Judge Tyler looked at Roger and loudly announced, "Overruled. What's good for the goose is good for the gander. Mr. Barklett, you opened the door when you inquired about the second set of killings."

Barb asked loudly, "Dr. Jones, didn't you also do the necropsy on the third set of killings?"

"Yes, I did. There was only one adult manatee killed on the third date."

"Sir, isn't it true that the cyanide in the darts from the second set of killings weren't located on the harpoon or carcasses from the third set of killings."

"That's true."

Barb looked at the jury and then the Judge as she said, "No further questions."

Buck Williams was sitting at the defense table and drawing pictures of flowers on one of Barb's legal pads. Cpl. Sanchez sat to his side watching the artwork while Sgt. Percersi sat next to the clerk's table and appeared to be nodding off.

Roger stood up and announced, "The State calls Doug Shearer."

After Doug was sworn in, Roger asked, "Please give us your name and profession."

"My name is Doug Shearer and I am a detective with the Lee County Sheriff's Office."

"What is your involvement in this case?"

"I was the investigator assigned to this case."

"Could you tell the jury what your investigation showed from the first set of killings?"

"As you know, the defendant was found with a newly dead manatee and a chainsaw that had blood samples from that dead manatee and two others that were discovered later that day. From this evidence, we concluded that the Defendant was involved in all three deaths. However, we ran into problems when we tried to reconstruct the crime. We did a series of tests timing how long it would take to run between the points where all of the manatees were found. We then did tests with the defendant's boat and found it was impossible that he could've been in all three spots and killed all three manatees without help. Unfortunately, we haven't found the people that've helped the defendant.

"Approximately, one month after the first set of killings, two more dead, headless manatees were found. However, there is no evidence, at this time, connecting the defendant to that crime.

"Three weeks after the second set of killings, which was one week ago, a third, beheaded manatee was found with a harpoon in his side. On the handle of the harpoon, a blood sample was found, which matched the defendant's. In addition, at a prior hearing, the defendant confessed that it was his blood."

"I have no further questions, your honor," Roger said.

Barb stood up and said, "I have a few questions, your honor. Detective, where was my client the night of the second set of killings?"

Doug felt his face turning red, "I don't know."

Barb asked, "Detective, after my client entered a plea of not guilty and bonded out of jail, didn't you think it was prudent to have him under surveillance?"

"We didn't anticipate any other killings."

"I think I understand your reasoning. But my next question is, why didn't you have the defendant under surveillance after the second set of killings?"

Doug hesitated, "I didn't think he would try something so bold. In retrospect, I wish we had."

Barb moved in for the kill, "Are you incompetent or just stupid?"

Roger jumped up, "Objection, argumentative."

Judge Tyler glared at Barb, "Sustained."

Barb looked at the jury and smiled, "No further questions, your honor."

Roger stood up and stated, "The State rests, your honor."

Judge Tyler looked over at the jury and said, "Ladies and Gentlemen of the jury, I want to thank you for your attention today. It's 4:30 p.m. and this is a good time to stop for the day. Please be back tomorrow at 9:00 a.m. sharp."

Sgt. Percersi stepped forward and motioned for the jury to follow him. As the jury walked between the counsel tables, Buck continued to draw pictures of flowers on Barb's yellow legal pads as Cpl. Sanchez patiently watched. After the jury left the courtroom, Judge Tyler looked at Barb and asked, "Does the defense have any motions?"

Barb stood up and said, "Yes, we do your honor. I would ask that the charges be dismissed because the state has not proved the elements of manatee harassment. The only thing they have proved is that my client was in possession of a dead manatee that was headless. They can't prove that my client had any contact with the manatee when it was alive. They can't prove that my client had anything to do with the manatee deaths."

141

Judge Tyler looked over at Roger as he stood up to rebut Barb's argument. Judge Tyler raised her hand and said, "Mr. Barklett, I don't need for you to respond to Ms. Brandon's arguments. They are so absurd that they don't even warrant a response." Judge Tyler turned toward Barb and said, "Your motion is denied."

Judge Tyler looked at Barb standing in front of her fuming over her public criticism. To Judge Tyler's delight, the media members were writing furiously after her comments. Finally, Barb broke the silence and said, "Your honor I would ask that you reconsider. I have some cases I would like to cite to the Court."

Judge Tyler stood up and raised her voice, "Counselors, I need to see both of you in my Chambers. Court is dismissed." Judge Tyler banged her gavel and walked toward her chamber door. Roger and Barb reluctantly followed the Judge into her chambers, as Sgt. Percersi and Cpl. Sanchez took Buck back to his holding cell.

Judge Tyler sat in her over-stuffed green office chair as Barb and Roger followed her in. Judge Tyler motioned for both of them to sit down and said, "Ms. Brandon, I'm concerned with your courtroom attire. Your blouse is cut low and your cleavage is not appropriate for the courtroom. I trust tomorrow you will dress more professionally."

Barb was beside herself with anger. She had worn her Blue Armani suit in front of Judge Tyler for over a year and she had never made a comment. It was too much for Barb, and she blurted out, "You've got to be kidding me. There's nothing wrong with this outfit. I've worn it before in your courtroom, and you've never said anything."

Judge Tyler raised her voice and said, "I don't like your attitude, counselor. Maybe I should report you to the Florida Bar. What do you think about that?"

Barb looked at her nemesis and said, "It didn't work the last time you reported me to the Bar; it won't work this time. However, I will promise you this. I'm going to report you to the

Judicial Qualifications Committee because of your personal attacks on me. I can't wait to get my complaint prepared and sent in."

Judge Tyler and Barb were glaring at each other as both of their faces turned red. The silence was very strained for Roger, and he finally said, "Judge, can I make a comment?"

Judge Tyler snapped her head towards Roger and said, "Shut up, needle dick!"

Roger's ears turned red, and he became lightheaded as he looked at Judge Tyler across the desk. He could see Barb out of the corner of his eyes, trying to hide her smile. Roger was at a loss for words and decided to get up and go back to the courtroom to avoid a confrontation. When Roger stood up, Barb quickly stepped in front of him and led the way toward the door. The silence in the room was deafening as Roger considered his options. He looked back over his shoulder and saw Judge Tyler smiling as he walked away. When he reached the door, he turned around and said, "Your honor, I think there's something you should know."

Roger smiled and continued in a playful voice, "It's not the size of the organ that matters, but the size of the auditorium it's played in."

Roger waited until the insult registered in Judge Tyler's eyes, and he quickly shut the door as he hurried back into the courtroom.

Chapter 22

The second day of the trial started with Sgt. Percersi bellowing, "All rise, the Honorable Brenda Lopez Tyler presiding."

Judge Tyler sat down and said, "Please, be seated. How does the defense wish to proceed?"

Barb stood up and announced, "Buck Williams is the only witness for the defense."

Judge Tyler said, "Mr. Williams, please raise your right hand to be sworn."

Buck was unsteady on his feet for a few seconds, but slowly raised his right hand. The clerk asked, "Do you swear to tell the truth?"

Buck looked at the clerk and said forcefully, "I most certainly do."

Buck smiled at the jurors as he walked toward the stand in his orange jumpsuit and white sandals. Once he was seated, he looked over towards his lawyer at the podium.

Barb asked, "Please tell us your full name and date of birth, Mr. Williams."

"My name is Buck Jacob Williams. I's born December 2, 1939."

"Where do you live?"

"I got my house out on Matlacha bay, but I've been a guest of the county for the past week."

There were a few snickers from the audience as Barb continued, "Mr. Williams do you have any family?"

"My wife's dead; we buried her a little over a year ago. I still got my son and daughter and my grandkids."

"Mr. Williams, did you hear Deputy Burns testify yesterday that he found you with a dead manatee that had its head missing?"

"Yeah, I heard him."

"Why were you around a dead, headless manatee?"

Buck sat up in his chair, looked around the courtroom and his gaze settled on his family. He smiled at them as the silent seconds ticked by. Finally, Judge Tyler leaned forward as she looked to her left with her one good eye and said, "You need to answer the question, Mr. Williams."

Buck looked to his right at the judge and said, "Judge, I'm gonna answer, but the truth might upset some people."

Judge Tyler replied, "Mr. Williams, I don't care who it upsets. Tell the truth."

Buck turned and looked at the jury for a few seconds and said matter-of-factly, "Ya know, his plan almost worked. I needed the money so I swallowed my pride. That's until that two-faced son of a bitch insulted my family and my people."

Buck stood up in the witness stand, pointed towards the *Save Our Seacows* group and yelled, "In that newspaper article, he said my people were worse than trailer trash. I don't give a damn about you insulting me, but when you talked about my people and my family; that's it. George Steinworth paid me to take the blame for this."

There was an immediate uproar in the audience and George Steinworth yelled out, "You are a goddamn liar. You're just trying to save your ass."

Judge Tyler banged her gavel repeatedly while she yelled, "Order. Order. Order in the court."

George Steinworth yelled, "I will not let this man slander me."

Judge Tyler yelled, "Sit down and shut up."

Sgt. Percersi walked towards Mr. Steinworth, and he reluctantly sat down next to his cousin. The other members of the *Save Our Seacows* were squirming with anger.

Doug and Roger looked at each other in amazement, while Barb had leaned forward on the podium for support. Cpl. Sanchez had unzipped her pepper spray pouch in case she had to control the defendant or the crowd. Judge Tyler turned towards

Buck and said in a quiet voice, "Please sit down and continue your testimony."

Buck's face had turned red and the veins in his skinny neck were noticeably pulsating. He sat down and leaned forward in his chair, looking at the jury. He continued, "I ain't killed no damn manatee. All I did was cut their heads off after Steinworth and his loverboy cousin shot 'em with a shotgun."

Mr. Steinworth's silver hair was disheveled as he stood up and yelled, "That's a lie."

Mr Steinworth's bald-headed cousin, Mitchell Brown, stood up next to him and tried to get him to sit down. Sgt. Percersi pointed at both men and yelled, "If youz two don't sit down, I'm gonna bounce ya. Sit down!"

Mr. Steinworth and his cousin reluctantly sat down with Sgt. Percersi standing over them. Judge Tyler banged her gavel three times and yelled, "Order in the Court."

Members of Buck's family were staring at the *Save Our Seacows* members. The red shirts of *SOS* were very quiet as they looked around the courtroom for some guidance. Judge Tyler looked back at Buck and said, "You may continue."

Barb finally broke out of her shock and said, "Objection, your honor. He's not being responsive to my questions."

Judge Tyler stood up and pointed her finger at Barb as she yelled, "Sit down and shut up before I find you in contempt of court."

Judge Tyler sat back down and said quietly, "You may continue."

Buck's hands started to shake and his voice cracked as he continued, "I just wanted a little money to pass on to my kids. I's never able to save anything for 'em. So I took it. I took the goddamn blood money from that snake in the grass."

George Steinworth jumped to his feet and yelled, "Judge, make him stop lying. I will not sit here and let him lie and slander my reputation."

As Judge Tyler banged her gavel, Buck stood up, pointed towards George Steinworth and shouted with every ounce of

146

energy in his body, "Why don't ya tell 'em how ya tracked the manatees down with your fancy computer? Why don't ya tell 'em why ya took the heads? And why...don't... ya..."

Doug and Roger watched in amazement as Buck Williams started to wobble. His eyes rolled back in his head and he fell forward. When Buck fell forward his torso hit the edge of the witness box, tumbling forward. The momentum of his body moving forward caused him to flip over the rail, head first and land on the court reporter, Mrs. Burnsmith. When Buck had flipped over the witness stand, his white sandals flew through the air and landed in the middle of the red shirts of *SOS*.

Mrs. Burnsmith was knocked off her stool and Buck was sprawled on the floor. The courtroom erupted with yells and screams as Doug rushed forward and looked at Buck. His eyes were rolled back in his head and his face was a gray pale. Doug felt his neck for a pulse, but there wasn't one. He looked up at Roger and shook his head negatively as Sgt. Percersi called for paramedics on his portable radio.

The screams and yells from Buck's family were slightly louder than the yells from the *Save Our Seacows* club. Cpl. Sanchez had hit the panic button on her beeper and reinforcements arrived to quell the angry people in the courtroom. Doug looked up and saw Steinworth talking to his cousin in a hushed tone. They got up and started to leave the courtroom. Doug jumped over the railing and grabbed them both as he said, "Not so fast, boys. I've got sworn testimony from a witness that you two were behind these manatee killings. I'm gonna have to detain both of you for questioning."

Doug, Roger and Cpl. Sanchez escorted George Steinworth to the state's witness room and put his cousin, Mitchell Brown, in the defense's witness room. Judge Tyler had given up on order in the courtroom, and she just sat back in her chair watching the fiasco while Sgt. Percersi stood guard in front of the bench with his gun holster unfastened.

Cpl. Sanchez guarded Mitchell Brown in the defense witness room while Doug and Roger went in the state's witness room to question George Steinworth. When Doug entered the room he said, "I need to take your statement, Mr. Steinworth."

"I will not give a statement until I talk to my attorney."

Roger tried to intimidate him and said, "Your attorney can't do nothin' for you. I'm the only one that can help. If you give me a statement, I'll let you go."

"I repeat, I will not give a statement until I talk to my attorney."

Doug and Roger were flustered as they went back outside. Doug asked Cpl. Sanchez if anyone had spoke to Mitchell Brown and was told no. As they were talking, Barb came up from behind and said, "Detective Shearer, I represent Mr. Steinworth. He's invoking his right to remain silent."

Doug turned to look at Barb and said, "It's a conflict of interest for you to represent Buck Williams and George Steinworth. One client can't testify against another. That's a conflict."

Barb gave Doug a smirk and said, "The paramedics told me Buck died of a massive heart attack. They said he was dead before he hit the ground. Since Buck's dead, I don't have a conflict. Mr. Steinworth is not giving a statement. Please arrest him or release him."

Doug walked over and opened the state's witness room and said to Mr. Steinworth, "You can go now. Your lawyer has invoked your right to remain silent."

Mr. Steinworth walked over to Barb and whispered in her ear. Barb spoke up, "I am also requesting that you release my other client, Mitchell Brown."

Roger said, "Sorry, it's a conflict of interest for you to represent Mitchell Brown. I'm going to give him immunity for his testimony. You can't get out of that conflict, Barb."

Roger and Doug walked towards the clerk's table as they left a shocked George Steinworth and his well-paid legal talent. Mitchell Brown was the needed link to verify Buck's amazing story. Doug and Roger approached Mrs. Burnsmith who was disinfecting her court reporter's machine at the clerk's table.

They convinced her to follow them in to record their conversation with Mitchell Brown. Doug and Roger quickly planned their strategy to get the information needed for the prosecution and conviction of George Steinworth.

Cpl. Sanchez opened the door and Doug, Roger, and Mrs. Burnsmith walked in. Mitchell Brown was a slender man dressed very sharply with pressed khaki pants and a brightly-colored madras shirt. He had a large gold chain hanging around his neck and a shiny Rolex on his wrist. He looked around quickly and said in a whining voice, "I don't wanna go to jail. Please, I've been to jail before. I don't do well in jail."

Roger turned a chair backwards, straddled it and sat down as he said, "Mr. Brown, if you tell the truth and agree to testify against George Steinworth, I will give you immunity and you won't go to prison. If you don't cooperate, we will convict you and ask the judge to give you 30 years in prison."

Roger hesitated and let the choice sink in. He then continued, "Do you understand your options?"

Mitchell Brown looked like a cornered animal and pulled his arms around himself as he said, "I understand. I'll cooperate."

Roger and Doug arranged the chairs around the small table while Mrs. Burnsmith set up her court reporter's machine.

Brown asked, "Do you mind if I smoke?"

Roger replied, "Go ahead."

Roger waited until Br. Brown had lit up and inhaled, "Mr. Brown, I want this to be on the record. That's why I have a court reporter here to record everything. Are you ready to start?"

Brown exhaled his smoke and said quietly, "Yes, I'm ready."

Roger began, "Do you swear to tell the truth?"

Brown said, "Yes."

Roger said, "In exchange for your truthful testimony today, I am giving you immunity for any crime you committed concerning these dead manatees. Do you agree to this?"

"Yes, I do."

Roger continued, "Give us your name and address."

"My name is Mitchell Brown and I currently live on Sanibel with George Steinworth. Although, I guess I'll be moving somewhere else after today."

"How are you and Mr. Steinworth related?"

Mr. Brown laughed quietly and said, "We're not. I met him about six years ago on a cruise. We hit it off and enjoyed each other's company, if you know what I mean. At the time, I was a bartender in Miami and lived in a fleabag apartment. So, at the end of the cruise he invited me to visit for a week with him here on Sanibel. I enjoyed my time with him, and I liked being wined and dined at the best restaurants on the island. At the end of the week, he asks me to move in with him. I sure didn't have anything else better in Miami, so I said yes.

"You know, people here on Sanibel are pretty conservative, so we decided that I would be his long lost cousin. For the past six years I've lived a life of luxury at George's house. Until today."

Roger asked, "Did you know Buck Williams?"

Mr. Brown continued, "Yes, I knew him. Back in the mid-nighties they passed the net-ban. Some of the former net fisherman started being fishing guides. A friend of George introduced us to Buck. A couple of times a year he would drive his old mullet boat to our dock, and he would guide us on a trip in George's Grady-White. We always caught fish with Buck.

"Well, about six months ago, Buck took us fishing and tells us that this'll probably be the last time because he'd been diagnosed with liver cancer. He says that the doctors tell him he has less than a year to live. You know, we're upset about hearing this. On the way home from fishing, George asks Buck if he would like to make some money for his family before he dies. Buck agreed, and once we docked, they sat down in the boat and cooked up this plot."

Roger asks, "What plot?"

Brown pointed his head towards the courtroom and said, "The manatee murders. George tells Buck he'll give him $25,000 in cash if he gets caught with a dead manatee and another $25,000 in cash if he testifies at trial that he was responsible for killing other manatees. George also promised him $5,000 a month in cash while he was alive to keep quiet in jail.

"Buck tells him he's got to sleep on it and think about it. He comes back the next day and says he'll do it if the money is delivered in cash to his daughter. So George comes up with this plan to track the manatees tagged with radio buoys on his portable lap-top computer. He gave Buck some money to go buy a heavy-duty chainsaw to cut off the manatee heads after he shot them with a shotgun."

Roger said, "Let me stop you there. Why did you chop off the heads?"

"George got this idea to create a fake demand for manatee brain so people would hunt the manatee. The more the manatees were hunted, the more the public would be outraged and allow more slow speed zones."

Roger scratched his head and said, "I don't understand. Mr. Steinworth has spent so much time and energy protecting the manatees that he loves. Why would he kill three manatees with a shotgun?"

Mr. Brown started laughing and said, "That's what you think. He hates the manatees. I guess when he was younger, one tipped his canoe over. He loves his damn canoes. That's why he started *Save Our Seacows.*

"He only used the manatee to get his own agenda passed. There were more and more motorboats around Tarpon Bay and he had to paddle over their wakes. He didn't like being disturbed when he canoed, so he used the manatee to get slow zones passed. He hates the manatees, but he loves to use them for his own purpose."

Roger looked at Doug and then asked Mr. Brown, "What did you mean by fake demand for manatee brain?"

Mr. Brown continued, "He got this idea to start the rumor that manatee brain was twice as potent as Viagara. George and I always traveled a lot. His favorite place is the Orient. He took

151

me to these high-dollar gentlemen clubs. They would eat endangered species like tigers and bald eagles for dinner. And then the straight guys would divide up with geisha girls and enjoy themselves. They were always looking for something to make them better lovers. Over in those clubs, those guys eat Viagara like candy.

"So, George gets this idea to take manatee brain and put it in the blender and liquify it. The reason he wanted to liquify it is that we put some cocaine, speed and Viagara in the blender with it. A small shot of it would give you a burst of energy. George is also a good marketer. The first batch of those three manatee brains we mixed up, boxed it in dry ice and sent to a friend of his in Tokyo. George paid $25,000 to the manager of the men's club to introduce the drink to his rich customers. At the same time, he paid $25,000 to a reporter at the Tokyo paper to print a story about manatee brain being the latest expensive novelty to help men be better lovers.

"All of a sudden, everybody wants manatee brains in the Orient. Some people down in Belize are hunting the manatees. It's just a matter of time before someone in Florida kills more and ships the brains to Tokyo. Supply and demand is a dangerous tool."

Roger could feel the hair on the back of his neck stand up but he asked, "What happened to the heads?"

Brown said, "Well, I don't really know. When we came in that night with the three manatee heads, I wasn't feeling good. The sight and smell made me sick. I went inside and showered. I took a valium, had a glass of scotch and passed out in the recliner watching TV. When I woke up in the morning, everything was cleaned up."

Roger and Doug looked at each other in disgust and shook their heads. Brown inhaled the rest of his cigarette and put it out in the tray. Roger continued, "What happened the night Buck was arrested?"

Brown took a deep breath and continued, "We had caught the first manatee the night before. We traced it using a GPS to

Chino Island. You know that small canal that goes in the middle of the island and branches out to each side?"

Both Doug and Roger nodded affirmatively as Brown continued, "George told me there used to be a ship yard with dry dock on the island in the fifties and sixties. He knew that's why it was deep there on the backside of Chino and the canal in the middle. We saw on the lap-top that it went up in the canal on a rising tide. So we placed a big net across the entrance. We just drank beer and waited for the tide to start going out. The manatee ran into the net and got tangled. We brought it to the boat and shot it in the head. We called Buck at home on his cell phone and he drove to us in his mullet boat. He cut the head off, secured the manatee by ropes and pulled it across the sound towards Buck key. We put the manatee head in a garbage bag and put it in the fish box, filled with ice. Buck pulled it into that hidden bay behind 'Tween Waters Resort. There's a small opening in the mangroves on Buck Key near Roosevelt Channel and it opens into a big bay."

Roger and Doug both nodded as Brown continued, "He hid it in the mangroves and left it 'til the following night. If someone caught him that night he was just going to confess to the one kill. But George wanted a second manatee to shock the public. So after Buck hides the dead manatee he calls us on his cell phone and we make plans for the following night. We had been tracking different manatees with the lap-top and the GPS. Some of the manatees liked going up McIntire Creek on a rising tide so we planned on going there the next night. Buck understood that night was going to be his last night of freedom. He was kind of emotional, but he was insistent on trying to help his family with the money.

"The following night we had Buck anchor at the mouth of McIntire Creek and act as a lookout. We went up the creek and put the net across a narrow part of it, sealing in the manatee we had already tracked on George's lap-top. We waited on the tide to turn and drank some beer. Sure enough, when the tide turned the manatee got tangled in the net and we shot her. Right after we shot her, her baby swam up to us; a bonus. We used the speargun to shoot her and pull her in. After we got both of 'em to the side of the boat we called Buck on the cell phone.

Buck drove down the creek and chopped off the heads with the chainsaw. We put the two heads in the fish box with the other head from the night before. The baby manatee we pulled into the boat and let it stay in the back of the boat. We untied the mother's carcass and let the tide take her. After that Buck was supposed to drive to Buck Key and pull out the hidden manatee carcass from the mangroves towards the channel. After that, he called the sheriff's office and reported that there was illegal netting in the area. After thirty minutes, he called us and said the cops hadn't come yet. George told him to call and report it again.

"Meanwhile, we left McIntire Creek and went back into Pine Island Sound. We drove north until we saw the power lines across the water and turned west following the deep water until we get to the back of Ding Darling. We beached the boat next to the dirt road that ends by the water. George gets out his diving knife and cuts a hole in the middle of the manatee body. It was about six inches across. After that we carried the bloody baby up to where the tourist drive on the main road. George places the body so a mangrove branch goes up through the hole and out of the body. He was proud of himself. I remember him saying, 'It kinda looks like Moby Dick impaled himself on the mast of the ship.'

"So by this time, I'm getting kinda sick with all the blood and guts. I wasn't worth a damn when we got back to Tarpon Bay. When I woke up in the morning, I turned on the TV and saw *The Manatee Murders* all over. It was kinda spooky. George had done it, and Buck had gone along with the plot for money. Every time we carried the cash to Buck's daughter she wouldn't say anything; she would just start crying. But she took the money."

Roger asked, "What about the second set of killings?"

Brown said, "George was so excited about the publicity from the first set of killings, he wanted more. We met with Buck and told him we were going to kill two more and if he confessed at trial, George would give him another five thousand. After that, we started tracking two manatees that would go into Shell Creek on the rising tide and go back out with the falling tide. One night it was high tide at two in the morning, so we put a big net across the mouth of the creek and went back into the creek and waited on the manatees. A couple of hours into the falling tide, we hear the nostril blow. We waited for them to pass us and then we turned on the engines and herded them into the net. We pulled the net in and shot them with the cyanide darts. We used the darts for two reasons. First, it was closer to a residential area and we didn't want anyone to hear. Second, George wanted to confuse the cops with a different weapon. He really enjoyed manipulating the system.

"After that, George got out the chainsaw and cut their heads off. Blood was everywhere when he put them on ice. After that, he untangled the net and let the dead manatees float with the tide towards the causeway. Once we got back to the dock, I went inside and George cleaned up."

Roger asked, "What about the last killing with the harpoon?"

Brown answered, "George was very pleased with that. It took a lot of planning. He was ecstatic when the federal government came in and declared all waters in Lee County a slow zone. He tried to think of a way to antagonize the feds. Once again, he talked to Buck. He offered him five thousand for a cup of his blood and another five thousand if he testified at trial he had killed the manatee.

"After Buck agreed, he cut his pinkie on his left hand, and gave George a cup of his blood for five thousand cash. After we put his blood in a thermos, we put it in the cooler. We were ready to set the trap.

We had been tracking one manatee that went into Punta Blanca Creek every night to rest. In the morning, it would swim out in to the river to eat. We used the same net and put it across a narrow part of the creek. We went uptide and roared the engines until we woke the manatee and herded him into the net. George put on gloves, grabbed the harpoon and stabbed the manatee. I pulled the rope on the harpoon close, and George shot the manatee in the head with his shotgun. He fired up the chainsaw and cut off the head, putting it on ice. After that, he took Buck's blood from the cooler and poured it on the end of the harpoon. He took out his dive knife and carved, 'Fuck the feds' on the right side. We cut the manatee loose and let the tide take him.

"Once we got back to the dock, I went inside and took a valium with some vodka while George cleaned the boat. I woke up the next morning and George was like a little kid at Christmas. He was watching the news reports and jumping up and down. I walked in and he got frisky. I told him I had a headache, but he didn't care. Whatever George wants, George gets."

Roger asked, "Anything else you want to add?"

Brown said, "Not really. Other than I'm really sorry this happened."

Roger looked at Mrs. Burnsmith and said, "I know you've had a long day, but I need Buck's testimony and Mr. Brown's testimony transcribed as soon as possible so I can present it to the judge for a search warrant."

Mrs. Burnsmith frowned and said, "I gave money to *Save Our Seacows*, and I'm mad as hell. You'll have the transcript on your desk within the hour and there'll be no charge for it. I want you to put that lying scumbag in prison where he belongs."

Chapter 23

At noon, Mrs. Burnsmith delivered the transcripts of Buck Williams trial testimony and Mitch Brown's sworn statement to Roger's desk at the State Attorney's Office. Roger and Doug had already prepared the search warrant request. The warrant gave a history of the case and referred to the transcripts as Exhibits "A" and "B". Once the transcripts were attached to the package, Roger and Doug walked it up to Judge Tyler's office and she signed the search warrant.

Roger and Doug took the signed search warrant and jumped in Doug's truck. They put the portable blue light on the dash and drove to Sanibel as fast as possible. Doug radioed the sheriff's office and gave orders for three deputies and a crime scene investigator to meet him at the tollbooth by the Sanibel Causeway. After Doug received confirmation, he radioed the Sanibel police department and requested a pair of backup officers join the group.

As they were driving down Summerlin Boulevard at 85 mph Doug asked, "What do you think we'll find?"

Roger considered the possibilities for a few seconds and then said, "I don't know. We might find a shotgun. We'll have a tech run tests on it for a trace of manatee blood. I'll bet Steinworth has thrown the gun in the saltwater or bleached it clean. I guess the next piece of evidence would be the boat. We'll have the tech run blood tests on the boat to see if we can find a trace of manatee blood. It's been a few months and who knows how many cleanings. I'll be surprised if it shows any manatee blood. I think our best bet is to see if the fiberglass on Steinworth's boat matches the shards found on two of the manatees."

Doug said, "I don't know about the shards. The only thing the lab could narrow it down to was that it came off a boat that was less than five years old. They couldn't narrow it down to a specific boat manufacturer. Still though, it would be some corroborating evidence with Buck's testimony and Brown's statement. What else do you think might be there?"

Roger shrugged and said, "Some criminals are stupid. We might find receipts of cash withdrawals or a ledger book with the payments to Buck's family. It would be nice to find a receipt for a shipment of manatee brain to Tokyo. Who knows?"

During the remaining ride to Sanibel, each man concentrated in silence about the pending search for evidence at Mr. Steinworth's house. As they approached the causeway they spotted the sheriff's cruisers and Sanibel police cruisers waiting for them on the side of the road. As they rode by, Doug radioed for them to follow. Nine minutes later they pulled into George Steinworth's drive at 3:00 p.m.

As they got out of the car, Mr. Steinworth and Barb Brandon walked out the front door and stood on the front porch. As Doug and Roger walked up the marble entrance to the bayfront mansion, Barb spoke first, "Well, that didn't take you long. Do you have a search warrant?"

Doug replied, "Yes, we do."

Doug handed it to Barb and waived for the others to follow him into the house. Doug looked back at Barb and asked, "Counselor, can I assume you and your client will stay here on the porch, out of our way? Or do I need to secure Mr. Steinworth with handcuffs?"

Barb confidently replied, "We'll be sitting here on the porch drinking lemonade."

The house was searched room by room by deputies. The crime scene investigator started on the Grady-White. Blood tests were conducted while Doug searched each and every compartment of the boat. After an hour, he was not able to find anything on the boat related to the manatees. Doug directed her to the garage to search for blood by using a luminal scan on any possible tool or knife that might have been used.

Doug walked back up to the house and found Roger, "Well, did anybody find anything."

Roger said in a frustrated voice, "A big goose egg. But they're still looking."

Doug looked through the kitchen window and saw Steinworth and Barb sitting in wooden rockers on the porch. He pointed towards them and said, "Let's go talk to them. They look a little too smug."

Roger followed Doug through the front door and walked down the porch to Barb and Steinworth. Barb watched them approach and asked, "Any success guys? My client would like to have his peace and quiet back on his property."

Doug pointed at Mr. Steinworth and said, "The only peace and quiet he's going to have is at the Lee County Jail. Maybe I can arrange for him to be in the same cell Buck Williams was in."

Barb laughed and said, "You're so cute when you're angry. You won't be able to arrest Mr. Steinworth. You have no credible evidence. You have zero physical evidence. Buck Williams is dead. Even though you could use his transcribed testimony for a search warrant, you can't use his testimony as evidence at trial. The Constitution gives you the right to confront your accuser in court. Your other star witness is Mitchell Brown. He has zero credibility."

Barb pulled out some papers from her briefcase, handed them to Roger and said, "Before Mr. Steinworth and I came out here, I stopped by my office and ran a criminal records check on Mr. Brown. You will notice that he has five convictions of insurance fraud and two convictions for grand theft. He doesn't sound like the most credible witness."

Barb smiled as Roger looked over the papers in silence. Doug was seeing red as he realized that Steinworth was trying to use his high-dollar attorney to squeeze through the cracks. Doug left Roger looking over the papers and went back inside and checked with his people for any new evidence. Doug walked through every room in the house one more time to see if he missed something. He finally walked out the back door towards the dock. As the sun was starting to set, he walked towards the end of the dock. Less than a month ago, he and Roger had been catching snook under the bright dock lights.

Doug was exhausted, so he sat down on the end of the dock, letting his legs swing freely. He could hear the deputies behind him going through their checklist. He knew the search was coming to an end with no new evidence. The only direct evidence against Steinworth was the testimony of his gay lover who had seven felony convictions. It was going to be an uphill battle to bring Steinworth to justice.

As Doug watched the sun fall, he heard the nostril blow of a manatee. He looked down the shoreline about 50 yards and saw a 10-foot manatee surface for air. The manatee went back under the clear, calm water but Doug could see it swimming towards him. The tail flume moving slowly displaced water in a rhythmic manner. The manatee surfaced about five yards from the dock and looked up at Doug. He kept his head above the water while swimming between the six crab buoys. The manatee nudged the buoy nearest Doug with his nose. The light bulb went off in Doug's mind and he jumped up. He grabbed the rope that was tied to the crab trap and pulled it up from bottom. As the trap surfaced, he could see half a dozen crabs crawling around the inside of the seaweed covered wire mesh. He pulled the trap up on the dock and unfastened the lid. Laying in the bottom of the trap was a manatee skull and mandible, bleached white by the elements.

Chapter 24

It was Friday afternoon and Doug was drinking beer in a quandary, sitting outside at his picnic table by the canal. Amanda's deadline of 6:00 p.m. was approaching or she was going back to Sarasota and financial security with her other suitor. Doug thought of his position with Amanda—she wanted to be married to someone who would love her and take care of her. He was one choice and her country club suitor, Trevor, was the other. Trevor had more money than Doug but was older. Doug remembered Amanda' favorite saying: "People that say money can't buy happiness just don't know where to shop."

Doug knew that Amanda enjoyed the attention and physical benefits of their relationship. But she didn't love Doug the way he loved her and they both knew it. But Doug didn't want to loose her. Heroin addicts called it their "cruel mistress." Doug understood how they felt.

Doug was watching a pod of dolphins swimming up his canal looking for lunch when his cell phone rang.

"Hello?"

"Hi Doug, this is Mary."

Doug could tell by her tone that this was not going to be a pleasant conversation but responded politely, "Hey, Mary. How are ya doing?"

"To be honest with you Doug, not good. I've been thinking about our relationship. I don't think it's heading anywhere. Don't you agree?"

Doug thought, *What a question! Sort of like—Are you still beating your wife?* He correctly thought that Mary's co-workers had been telling her that she needed a new man. Doug liked dating Mary but was not ready to settle down. He thought for a few seconds and said, "I enjoy your company, Mary. I feel very comfortable around you. I don't know where this relationship is heading; I kinda like it where it is."

"I bet you do! You call me whenever you want and come to my house for sex. You have no commitment but you get the benefits of a relationship!"

Exactly, thought Doug, but he said, "It seemed to me that you enjoyed our time together."

"Well, yes. But I need something more. I'm 32 and I want to have children. You need to think about us this afternoon. I've had a guy I know ask me out; he's nice and wants a family. If our relationship isn't going anywhere, I need to start dating other people. I'm going to happy hour with my girlfriends downtown at *The City Tavern*. I'll be there 'til seven. If you think there's a future to our relationship, you meet me there. If you don't come, I'm going out with other people."

Doug felt the pressure increasing in his ears and said slowly, "That's a lot to lay on someone at once; let me think about."

Mary's tone turned chilly, "You know what, this is turning into a minute-rice moment. I think I already know your answer, but you might surprise me. Goodbye."

Doug heard the click of the phone and felt his shoulders sag. He stumbled to his feet and walked back inside to the refrigerator for another cold beer. He opened the beer, took a long swallow and walked over to his stereo, turning it on to his favorite country music station. Doug sat down in his recliner and considered his situation. How ironic it was that both of the women in his life wanted to marry. Neither one had said anything about their love for Doug. Amanda wanted to wed for security and Mary wanted to marry so she could have merry kids at Christmas.

After a few minutes of thought, Doug picked up his phone and dialed Roger at the State Attorney's Office. After talking to the receptionist, he was put through to Roger.

"Hello Doug, what's up?"

"Hey Roger, let's go snook fishing tonight; it's full moon and I don't have anything better to do."

About the Author

John D. Mills is a fifth generation native of Ft. Myers, Florida. He grew up fishing the waters of Pine Island Sound and it is still his favorite hobby. He graduated from Mercer University in Macon, Georgia with a BBA in Finance and worked briefly for Lee County Bank in Ft. Myers. He returned to Macon and graduated from Mercer's law school in 1989.

He started his legal career as a prosecutor for the State Attorney's Office in Ft. Myers. In 1990 he left the State Attorney's Office and began his private practice specializing in Criminal Defense and Personal Injury law. His first novel, *Reasonable and Necessary*, was published in 2000.